Christoph

Plays

Other P(
The Coming ......u
Where Do We Live
Dying City

Other People: 'the secret of Shinn's success is the way he exploits the dramatic gap between what is said and that which is left unsaid . . . Writing like this is rare' *Independent*

The Coming World: 'A piece that tackles big themes – the nature of truth and of love – with a deceptively light touch. In its final moments, Shinn creates a sense of loss and lost opportunities that is deeply affecting' *Daily Telegraph*

Where Do We Live: 'Shinn successfully evokes a wary, troubled Lower Manhattan peopled by characters who speak arresting dialogue' *The Times*

Dying City: 'In his achingly beautiful new play . . . Shinn's achievement is to have written a drama of rare delicacy in which politics are not in the character's mouths, but in their circumstances and lives' *Variety*

Christopher Shinn was born in Hartford, Connecticut and lives in New York. His plays include *Four*, *Other People*, *Where Do We Live*, *What Didn't Happen*, *The Coming World*, *On the Mountain*, and *Dying City*. He is the winner of an OBIE in playwriting and a Guggenheim Fellowship in Playwriting. He teaches playwriting at the New School for Drama, New York.

To my directors

CHRISTOPHER SHINN

Plays: 1

Other People
The Coming World
Where Do We Live
Dying City

with an introduction by the author

Methuen Drama

METHUEN DRAMA CONTEMPORARY DRAMATISTS

First published in Great Britain in 2007

1 3 5 7 9 10 8 6 4 2

Methuen Drama
A & C Black Publishers Limited
38 Soho Square
London W1D 3HB
www.acblack.com

ISBN-10: 0 713 68327 9
ISBN-13: 978 0 713 68327 1

A CIP catalogue record for this book is available from the British Library.

Typeset by SX Composing DTP, Rayleigh, Essex
Printed and bound in Great Britain by Bookmarque Ltd, Croydon, Surrey

Contents

Christopher Shinn:
Chronology of first performances

Four	(Royal Court Theatre, London)	1998
Other People	(Royal Court Theatre, London)	2000
Other People	(Playwrights Horizons, New York)	2000
The Coming World	(Soho Theatre, London)	2001
Four	(Manhattan Theatre Club, New York)	2002
Where Do We Live	(Royal Court Theatre, London)	2002
What Didn't Happen	(Playwrights Horizons, New York)	2002
Where Do We Live	(Vineyard Theatre, New York)	2004
On the Mountain	(South Coast Rep, Costa Mesa, California)	2005
Dying City	(Royal Court Theatre, London)	2006
Dying City	(Lincoln Center, New York)	2007

Introduction

In late 1997, I was a few months out of school. My play *Four* had been rejected by every major theatre in America, and I had no real prospects to speak of. But I began a new play called *Other People* nevertheless.

I had recently been to see *Shopping and Fucking* at New York Theatre Workshop. I felt it was one of those plays that valorizes the thing it claims to critique, and derives its popularity from just that guilt-relieving contradiction (you can enjoy the nihilistic sex on display as long as the playwright makes you feel ashamed of yourself for it). My undergrad teacher Tony Kushner had put the idea into my head that playwrights can respond to plays they hate by writing new ones – I think he even told me he wrote *Angels in America* in response to some stupid AIDS play. So I set out to write a play about what I was feeling at the time – that nihilistic dramas dealing with emotional pain were being celebrated by a culture that didn't have time for more run-of-the-mill suffering. To be seen, it seemed to me, hurt had to be sexualized, aestheticized into something cool. I wanted to expose the cultural imperative to make suffering hip, to argue that it was not inherently so.

I was really hurting then. Not like the Lower East Side denizens of *Rent* (another show I wrote *Other People* in response to) – I had a nice Lower East Side apartment – but like the characters, say, in a Chekhov play, for whom an inherent and inexorable longing is as much a problem as any kind of external authority, economic system, or conventionality is. In fact, I believe I read *The Seagull* on the night I began writing *Other People* in earnest – New Year's Eve, 1997. I wanted to examine my loneliness, which I felt was determined not only by capitalism, not only by the shallow alternative culture that rebelled against it, but by my own conflicting desires as well. I was interested in finding an internal solution to my unhappiness, alongside investigation of forces outside of myself. What others in my world were doing – throwing up their hands at the awesomeness of what confronted them and embracing

apathy and ennui – I had to reject, because I was so
hopeful, so desperate, for a better life.

I wrote the play quickly, with a certainty that it would
never be done. I felt this not just because I had no career, or
because the culture seemed so antipathetic to my point of
view, but because I was a wreck at the time – I couldn't
really fathom any kind of future for myself. I was living on
student loans, smoking two packs a day, I had terrible
relationships. I was writing just to survive psychically, with
very few practical considerations. Then, in the fall of 1998,
the Royal Court saved me from my aimlessness by
producing *Four* in their Young Writers' Festival. Richard
Wilson gave me a simple, truthful production, Michael
Billington and David Benedict gave me raves – all of a
sudden, I had a career! Then in 2000 the Court did *Other
People*, in a remarkably honest production directed by
Dominic Cooke. This is where I met the incredible Daniel
Evans, who would go on to star in the sequel to *Other People*,
Where Do We Live.

I wrote *Where Do We Live* in late 2001. Why did I write this
play? In the fall of 2001, my father was dying, I had been
through a devastating break-up . . . and instead of dealing
with my pain, I tried to escape it by being very social. But
just as with the time before *Other People*, I kept seeing things
in my community that bothered me. Everyone – myself
included – seemed so terrified and disdainful of feelings, in
themselves and in art. Then 9/11 happened, the most awful
thing, its awfulness in no need of elaboration here. The
suspension of social ritual in the aftermath gave me an
excuse to stay in my room and look out the window at the
empty space where the towers used to be, to write and
mourn and not call anyone back, to think about how I had
arrived at such an unhappy place. With all this time to
meditate, what was undeniable to me was that actually I had
made very little progress since *Other People* in coming to
terms with my feelings, my values, my conflicting desires:
while I maintained a critical stance towards my community,
I realized I was also deeply implicated in it, still looking to it

for satisfactions, rewards, attention, love. And although I
had told myself that what distinguished me from others in
my community was that I was looking inward to address
problems of emotional pain, I hadn't seen many results from
this supposed self-scrutiny. While I felt I was more or less
maintaining my sense of self, someone who was truly in
touch with himself would not have been in the community I
was in in the first place. *Where Do We Live* was a big first step
in recognizing who I really was – a hypocrite.

Shortly after I finished the play my father died. A few
months later I went to London, where Richard Wilson gave
me an elegant and sensitive production in the round in the
Theatre Upstairs.

My first play about twins, *The Coming World*, was written
after *Other People* and before *Where Do We Live*. But in a sense
that's not so. I have since changed the play from the version
produced at the Soho Theatre. I didn't actually see it there
– one of my great regrets. It was early in rehearsals in the
spring of 2001 when the aforementioned break-up
happened and my dad's leukemia worsened, and I went
back to New York, the stress of London being too much. I
knew I had to go home when I was on the Tube one
afternoon, and a mentally ill man who was inexplicably
carrying four or five supermarket chickens glared at me and
muttered, 'You're a piece of shit. You're a piece of shit.'
The whole car turned and looked at me. He was right, that's
how I felt. *I am a piece of shit*, I thought. But I mustered the
last of my strength and replied, 'No I'm not.' Then he threw
one of the chickens at me.

I know that many people were deeply moved by *The
Coming World* in the form in which it was seen at the Soho.
I'm lucky that Mark Brickman, the gorgeous Doraly Rosen,
and Andrew Scott did such great work in my absence. I
hope the changes I've made to the play have helped it.
While its basic shape and thematic concerns are the same, I
feel that the critics who said it was overwritten were right. It
needed editing. But the heart of it remains: three souls on a
beach in a working-class American town attempting to deal

with an ineffable pain. The nascent dilemma of *Where Do We Live* is present in a more stark form here: of the two brothers, one is an introvert who has rejected the hypocrisy of his community by withdrawing deep into himself, and the other is an extrovert who tries to exploit the empty and cynical culture he's in, to wring as much pleasure and power out of it as he can. At the time, this must have seemed to me the only two options available for living in the world: rejection or submission. Was there anything in between? Dora has a hand in both worlds, aware of an inner life that promises access to deeper truths but also an unbearable isolation. The play is about her struggle to make up her mind about which world to live in, the inner one or the outer one. The choice she makes is the one I was still making then: the choice not to make a choice, the choice not to look more deeply.

I would come back to twins – and the amazing Andrew Scott – with *Dying City*. I wrote it following the American premiere of *Where Do We Live,* which I directed at the Vineyard Theatre in New York in May 2004. I loved directing and hoped to work again with two wonderful actors from that production, Luke Macfarlane and Emily Bergl. *Where Do We Live* had been a big play – nine actors, a dozen scenes, multiple locations – and I had a fantasy of a stripped-down rehearsal process: two actors, one set, and me. So I set out to write a play for the three of us. I was very concerned at the time with America's war in Iraq. I had marched against the war and was quite certain that the Bush administration was not equipped to carry it out. But I also diverged from many in my community in feeling that in theory the war was defensible. I never supported *this* war, and I certainly did not approve of the handling of it; but I could imagine a war in Iraq that I would support, for reasons having to do with human rights, the very worthy fight against oppression.

When I began thinking about the play I commenced a psychoanalysis, which put me in touch with very hateful and destructive feelings in myself, of a far greater power than I had ever intuited. Very quickly I understood that to write a play about violence I would have to face, at long last, the violence in myself – what I had been at once approaching and backing away from in the protagonists of my previous plays. To keep things close to home, to limit any attempt to escape or avoid my conflicts after a lifetime of flight, I set the play in an apartment like my own, looking out on the same downtown skyline I look out on each day as I sit and write. I imagined that every character was an aspect of myself. This play was going to confront me with myself or it was going to be nothing.

Writing it was an agony. I don't exaggerate when I say that at times I thought it would kill me. My hair changed color while I was working on it (everyone thought I'd dyed it, and it doesn't take a Freudian to note the play on words), and there were whole weeks when my heart rate remained so elevated that I thought about going to the emergency room. When I finished the play, I sent it to the Royal Court, because I felt it was too bleak to get on quickly in America. James Macdonald's extraordinary production bravely matched the spirit in which the play was written. Andrew Scott played the twins as two boys in a fit of warded-off grieving, and Sian Brooke gave a performance of astonishing contradictions, suffusing Kelly with both warmth and rage, suspicion and denial.

I don't think *Dying City* will be the last play I write that explores the centrality of hate in human life. I continue my psychoanalysis, and I continue to feel a profound confusion about the violence in the world and the violence in me.

Other People

Other People was first performed at the Royal Court Jerwood Theatre Upstairs, London, on 17 March 2000. The cast was as follows:

Petra	Doraly Rosen
Stephen	Daniel Evans
Mark	James Frain
Man	Nigel Whitmey
Tan	Neil Newbon
Darren/Waiter	Richard Cant

Director Dominic Cooke
Designer Robert Innes Hopkins
Lighting Designer Johanna Town
Sound Designer Paul Arditti

Characters

Stephen, *mid-twenties*
Petra, *mid-twenties*
Mark, *mid-twenties*
Tan, *late teens*
Man, *thirties/forties*
Darren, *mid-twenties*

Depending upon the actor's versatility, **Darren** and **Man** can be played by the same person; he also plays the **Waiter** in Act One, Scene Two.

In the original production, there was an interval after Act Two, Scene Three

Setting

New York City's East Village.

Time

Act One: a few days before Christmas, 1997.
Act Two: Christmas Eve, 1997.
Act Three: New Year's Eve, 1997.

Act One

Scene One

Hip restaurant, distant techno.

Petra People tell me this is really good, so.

Stephen Yeah?

Petra No, you look a little – I was wondering if you –

Stephen No, I'm, I guess I'm a little nervous.

Petra Yeah, you're nervous?

Stephen We talked on the phone, you know, and he sounded – he sounded – how did he sound? – he said – I don't even remember practically, I was so – nervous. We had a kind of – it was a distant conversation, he said how excited he was to leave the, you know, the clinic, and how much it meant for us to take him in, you know. He talked a little about the movie, which, Christ, the phone has been ringing off the *hook* for him, these movie people calling every half an hour – Anyway, whatever, I'm just, let's not talk about it, I'll just get more nervous. Why isn't he here yet? Let's not talk about it.

Petra Okay. They say the food is really good, really clean food. I can eat here.

Stephen It's just this music, you know.

Petra This music, yes.

Stephen You know?

Petra Well, it can't be helping your nerves.

Stephen And this crowd is a little precious, look, over there – don't look, she's looking here – there, now, that's my editor, right there, in the, whatever, that incredibly boring Donna Karan – see? – the black? –

Petra   I see –

Stephen   – who assigned me four new *blurbs* to do this
week because so-and-so had a family emergency, so I have
to write these movie reviews now and I was supposed to not
have another assignment till after – Oh wait: is this, do you
hear this? – is this a techno version of 'O Holy Night?' Oh,
blecch!

Petra   Christmas.

Stephen   Christmas. And these waiters, hello, heil Hitler,
master-race blondies, I bet they all run into each other at
the same auditions.

Petra   You're very nervous, Stephen.

Stephen   I know, and I told myself I wouldn't – hearing
his voice – you know – I just wish he'd get here because –
there's this *anxiety*, I mean – part of me, eight months later
part of me really has *forgotten* even what he looks like – and
to think he will go from this incredible abstract force in my
memory to this *physical*, undeniable *presence* – and that – and
that I don't really *know* him now – on the phone when we
. . . I think I'll have a drink.

Petra   You're allowed to have a drink.

Stephen   Blather blather.

Petra   Can I ask you a question?

Stephen   Of course.

Petra   Are you still in love with him?

Stephen   No. *No.* I mean, I recognize, you know, we were
never really in love, we were in, in *need*, or something,
something passed *between* us, and it was *genuine*, but it was not
– not by a long shot not – and I know that. No. But Mark
and I have never really talked about – and perhaps we
should have before I agreed to let him stay with us – but he
sounded so – what was I going to say to him? He needs
support now, after, you know, what *happened*. We'll talk

about it. We'll talk about it. It'll be okay. It'll be *okay*, it will, it just – things are – *different*. Now. I mean, you know? I'm barely used to you being back here, two days, and now . . .

Petra   I understand.

Stephen   Yeah . . . You are back. Which is wow. Go on, go, say something in Japanese for me.

Petra   No.

Scene Two

Mark *has joined the two.*

Stephen   Because, no, listen: when you guys were away, endless misery for the first six months, incessant, but this one night, like less than two months ago, I had this epiphany, this total – Can we even get some bread while we're – Mark, do you want any bread? I'll get the waiter.

As **Stephen** *looks around, signals:*

Petra (*to* **Mark**)   I can't eat bread, the carbohydrates – they did studies –

Stephen   Anyway so, this guy. The date. Cafe, nice, blah blah, we swap stories, walk around the East Village, blab about ex-boyfriends, look at some clothes, decide, what the hell, let's go see a show! So we go to the half-price booth, we go to this musical, musical's over, so we go – Darren – *Darren*'s his name – so the show lets out, we go for a drink. Now this will sound banal, mundane, but – we're in the bar – and I start to tell Darren about this *grant* I'm applying for for this *play* I've written – and by the way I'm nervous because I should be hearing if I got this grant or not before the new year, so keep your eye out in the mail – anyway – I tell him how I had just gotten so frustrated with my *job* and how I'd stopped even going on *auditions* because the stuff I was sent out for was so *wretched* and so how I decided to write a *play* – you know, and when you guys left I went back into therapy – and I'm just beginning to really *figure out* my patterns, you know, just, *pathological* sex and and this really degraded self-loathing 'love' instinct, I mean not-love but – but – I'm lonely, you know? You guys are – I'm kind of hating my life still and – I'm really *hot* for this guy actually, I mean he's *totally* – he has this weirdo pseudo-British accent sort of, he's a musician, he's got this really sexy, like, *detachment* going on, this really careless *swagger* and *ambivalence* –

Petra   A million years, he tells a story.

Stephen   Okay, okay: so I tell him about the grant and the play and he says he wants to read it. 'I'd really like to read it, Stephen. Sounds totally cool.' But I feel – I feel *weird*. I feel *something's off here*. Because – and I realize – I turn around briefly because I realize something about his *gaze* – he's not quite looking at me, he's sort of just looking *above* me, above my shoulder, and he's been fixed there the whole – and so I look behind me and I see that – and my heart – *breaks* – I see that he's watching the TV – above the bar. As he's talking to me. The – so I say, 'Derek? Derek?' And he says, 'Hold on.'

Petra   Darren or Derek his name is?

Stephen   He, whatever – 'Hold on.' And it's not – the show is like *Entertainment Tonight* but not, it's like a lighter version of *Entertainment Tonight*, they're interviewing some blonde woman, some *sitcom*, and I turn back around and I start to say something else, you know, and he says, 'One more sec.' *One more sec.* And. And so. I mean that's it.

Petra   So the story ends you went to bed with him.

Stephen   No! No he asked me to go home with him and I just said – 'Not tonight but I'll call' or whatever. Because, you know, because I *saw* at that moment – I understood – I thought: *How many of the people I've slept with have actually looked at me?* And I decided no, I decided, I will not go to bed with anyone for the rest of my *life* who I do not perceive has at

the very least an *interest in me as a human being*. You know, as a
separate person. Because – you know? There I am, sitting
before him, a real – TV – me – and he picks – because *no*.
Because that will not be my life. Anymore. Where's the
bread? The service here, seriously. It's a postmodern
restaurant, like, the waiters are just actors acting the role of
waiters but really aren't waiters and if you were hip enough
to understand it you'd enjoy yourself. You're not going
home for Christmas, are you, Petra?

Petra   No, oh no, my parents think I'm still in Japan and
I'm not about to – so if they call, you know, don't –

Stephen   Yeah, I'm not going home either, first time too,
this year I am standing *up* for myself. Because it would be
self-loathing to go back there. My play I'm working on, it's
actually about, it's about these certain events, this thing that
happened in my hometown, this really, this *beautiful* and
devastating thing actually – but – I'll tell you about it but I'm
talking a lot. What about you, Mark? What are you doing
for Christmas?

Mark   I'll be here.

Pause.

Stephen   Well. Well then, we are going, we are going to
have a fabulous Christmas I've decided.

Petra   I'm glad you decided that, ha.

Stephen   We will!

Petra   I know, I know, I'm just teasing.

Waiter *drops a basket of bread on the table.*

Petra   Well.

Stephen   Bravo.

Stephen *reaches for the bread.*

Mark   Can we say grace first?

Stephen *and* **Petra** *look at* **Mark***.*

Mark   I'd like to say grace.

Stephen   I think it'd be a first for this place. We're in Dante's fifth ring and you want to say grace.

Mark *bows his head.*

Mark   God, bless You for this food before us, and bless those less fortunate, those in pain, those in hunger, those in need of Your beauty and Your bounty. Amen.

Petra/Stephen   Amen.

A beeper goes off. **Mark** *checks, shuts it off. He takes a piece of bread.* **Stephen** *follows.* **Petra** *sips water.*

Scene Three

Apartment. Stage right living room, homemade wall center, stage left **Stephen***'s bedroom, far right wall is small kitchen unit, hall off leading to* **Petra***'s bedroom, upstage of kitchen unit is door leading to tiny bathroom and shower. Living room: a couch, a bookshelf, coffee table, small entertainment system.* **Stephen***'s bedroom: loft bed, small desk, boxes. Windows stage right look out on street, stage left windows look out on brick.*

Lights rise on **Stephen** *on his loft bed,* **Mark** *on the couch on the phone.* **Petra** *emerges from her room, bundled up in a long coat.*

Mark   – Well, yeah. I can come in, well. Um. You should.

Petra *exits the apartment.* **Stephen** *looks up from his bed.*

Mark   Well, like I said, I'll have to. Oh? Well, I suppose this is all. Great, especially for. Well, I can come in I can. Anytime. Okay. That's fine. But like I said. Till I see it. Okay. Yeah. Till I. Well, that's great that people are. But like I said. Okay. Okay that's fine. Okay. Bye.

He hangs up the phone. He opens up a book. **Stephen** *climbs off his loft bed, grabs his coat from the closet, enters the living room.*

Stephen   Hey.

Mark   Oh. Hi.

Stephen   Hey, thanks again for dinner.

Mark   Oh. You're welcome but. I have all this money.

Stephen   Yeah. I was gonna – oh, whatcha reading?

Mark   The Bible.

Stephen (*laughs*)   Ha. (*Stops.*) Oh – the Bible, really?

Mark   The Good Book.

Stephen   The Good News Bible.

Mark   The King James version.

Stephen   Right. Right. Um. Well, I was going to go down to the deli and get myself a Snapple or – how are you feeling, you want anything?

Mark   I'm fine.

Stephen   Snapple has this new peach juice which is – anyway, I'm just, I'm just going to *say* this however foreign to my nature it is to speak *directly*, *honestly*, you know, but, that's one of the things I've been working on, so. So. I just: I want to know you're okay. I guess. You've been really quiet, and . . .

Mark   I'm fine. Really. I know I'm. I know this is. Different. Unlikely even.

Stephen   Well, yeah! Very – it's definitely a – *new you* here, ha.

Mark   With the help of the Lord, yes. A new. Me.

Pause.

Stephen   I'm just, I'm a little uneasy, it's been so long, you know, and I feel a little – *lost* with you – and of course, our history, you know, and – your coming back here without our discussing – what's really *happened* in the – in the

time you've been – gone – *you* – you not being something
we've discussed and why – when you could stay anywhere
why – I mean I knew it was a rough time so I didn't want to
push but – now – just to know – what's going through your
head.

Mark   Right. Well. I think you'll find I tend to be more –
silent and not. Interested. In the past. Because. It causes me
pain to think about it. My life is about. The new me. In so
many ways. In this way (*holds up the Bible*) especially.

Stephen   Right. Right, well. And that's great, that's what
you needed to – recover. And I understand, I guess I'm just
being selfish, you know Petra's the same way: she was in
Japan for over half a year, you know, stripping, and she's
finally given it up, you know, she saved a lot of money and
she's come back so now she has money to write and to – do
what she wants without having to – you know, and which is
great – and she's the same, not wanting to – *talk*, to *define*
herself based on – so. So. It's hard for *me* but I understand.

Mark   The past is – bad news. It's only good news now.
For me. And thank God. Thank God.

Stephen   Right, sure. It's just so – different. But – well –
hell, you know – maybe we're all – getting it together, which
is great. Like our apartment is about *health*, you know, *healthy*
living – we're all – being *proactive* – not to sound not to
sound New Agey but . . .

Mark   You don't sound New Agey.

Stephen   Right, well, we're making *improvements*.

Mark   Absolutely. God bless us. It's not easy. This world.

Stephen   Yeah! Yeah, and I guess, and it doesn't have to
be now, I guess though I just hope we will you know
eventually have a chance to *talk*, really *talk*, about the past
year and – you know? just to – and – well, maybe I thought
– I'd feel better if I – if we – hugged, I mean we haven't –

because – I do love you, not, not in the past way but in this new way, you know?

Mark   Change is traumatic. It will take getting used to. The past me, Stephen. That's someone else. Have faith in. This me. Have faith in me now and know all will. Will be all right.

Stephen   Right.

Mark   I'll give you a hug.

Stephen   Good.

Mark *stands, hugs* **Stephen** *briefly, breaks the hug.*

Mark   You're my only friend. Only true, real friend in this world. I was too terrified to go at it alone, to jump back into the. Real world. Without you. God bless you. I say prayers of thanks that I am here with you.

Stephen   Right, right, well, great.

The phone rings.

Mark   Oh, give me some peace! Let the voicemail get it.

Stephen   Who are these, are these the movie people?

Mark   Yes. Oh Stephen. I have the option – because most of what was used ended up being mine – of putting my name on the film. Which I haven't – seen. This is. A dilemma.

Stephen   Oh.

Mark   They're sending me the cut. It doesn't really matter. The Lord will guide me.

Stephen   Right. Um – well, I have to get going on these *blurbs* I – I hope I didn't – upset you or – I just get neurotic, still, I hate it.

Mark   Then give it up. Release yourself to the Holy Spirit. What's 'neurotic'? What is that? Hand it to God, He'll know what to do with it. It won't be easy. But you can do it.

Stephen   Yeah. Yeah. God, it's a Marianne Williamson
moment! Right – well – you're probably right. I'm just – so
proud of you. And Petra. And glad you'll be getting to know
each other, I always kept you two apart, I kept my life so
compartmentalized before, you know. Well, I'll let you get
back to your reading. God, when I was a kid, I was into this
totally weird Wiccan stuff – Anyway. You want anything
from the deli?

Mark   I don't need anything.

Stephen   Okay.

He goes to the door.

Um. And just – anytime you need anything. Anything. I am
here for you.

Mark   Thank you.

Stephen   Anything at all. Just knock on my door. Anytime
no matter what. I want you to be well.

Mark   I will be. And God bless you.

Stephen   Right. Okay. Just – wanted to say that. So. Off
to get my Snapple!

Stephen *goes.* **Mark** *opens the Bible.*

Scene Four

Petra, *in a red gown, sits at a small table with a* **Man**. *Music.
Drinks.*

Petra   Oh now, this is fantasy.

Man   Petra, I swear to God. During office hours.
Countless girls. Sliding their leg against mine or hiking up
their – literally coming onto me like I can't tell you. It was
this basic business class I was teaching. Yeah.

Petra   No, I don't believe you, no: countless?

Man   Are you in college?

Petra   No.

Man   Graduate.

Petra   Yes.

Man   Where did you go to school?

Petra   Twenty questions we're playing here.

Man   Okay. What was your major?

Petra   Clearly, I mean, you're smiling like something's going on in that brain of yours, so what are you getting at?

Man   Well, you're smart, you're perceptive, maybe I've a little theory I'm working on. Acting?

Petra   Oh God please, say anything but that.

Man   Well then. No. Okay. But you did this to pay for school, you danced?

Petra   I had a scholarship, a very substantial scholarship, but not nearly enough to live on, and I knew that this was the only thing I could –

Man   Creative writing.

Petra   Who have you been talking to? Which girl? Joanna?

Man   Joanna, no. Joanna gives handjobs.

Petra   I don't.

Man   Whoa! I didn't ask you if you did, I wasn't asking you to, I was telling you, no, I don't care to talk to Joanna. I like you. I want to hear you talk about your interesting life. I say that without irony. I mean it: you, you are interesting to me.

Petra   Listen, I had a poetry professor at NYU –

Man   Ahh, NYU girl.

Petra   – no, listen: National Book Award this man won, and constantly, *constantly* asked me out to have 'beer' with him, a 'beer'. I said I don't drink. Said why don't we go 'work out' together. You believe this? Oh, no, I don't work out I say. Office hours: tells me my poems give him *erections*. Tells me he graded my poems, hands me the paper says, see this, this is my cum on your poems, guess I gotta give you an A plus. I am – I am eighteen years old, I am from Queens, my father doesn't barely know how to *write* or *read* and here is Mr National Book Award . . . and my father was a decent man, he was – he was the kind of man who calls radio call-in shows and says I'm a white man and I can tell you that whites are still racist against blacks. So I know this is wrong, this man is *wrong*. But I am stunned and can barely move – I am smiling – I have no idea what to *say*. So he makes a joke, whatever, and I say, okay, and I gotta go, and I get an A plus in the class. And I'm eighteen years old. So you're telling me girls are pulling up their *skirts* and – no. And if this is so, this is depressing.

Man   See, the class I taught was a night class and maybe those girls tend to be more desperate. But hey, I always said no. I did. So if you stripped to get through school, and you went over to Japan and made a lot of money, what uh, why are you doing it now? What's the reason now?

Petra   Well, what do *you* think? Why don't *you* tell me. Ha.

Man   No, no, I know I've been talking a lot. But I really want to know from you.

Pause.

Petra   Listen, I'm sorry, I'm just a little uncomfortable here, I think maybe you should talk with one of the other girls.

Man   No, please. Here.

He puts down a fifty-dollar bill on the table.

Please.

She stops for a moment. Then goes, off.

Scene Five

The apartment. Dark. **Mark** *sits on his couch-bed, under covers, the phone pressed to his ear. Door opens,* **Petra** *enters, tired.* **Mark** *hangs up the phone, door slams shut.*

Mark (*quietly*)   Hey.

Petra   Oh, I didn't wake you up, did I?

Mark   No. I baked some cookies, couldn't sleep. Want one?

Petra   Oh, I don't eat carbohydrates or sugar.

Mark   I'm sorry.

Petra   Me too, ha. But sugar, I think it makes you depressed, it's not widely known. And carbohydrates turn to sugar – so I'm doing an experiment of cutting it out.

Mark   Good for you, Petra.

Petra   But, I have this job interview in the morning so I should go to sleep. Stephen asleep?

Mark   Before you go to sleep, I made you this.

He hands her a card.

Petra   Oh, you made this yourself?

Mark   I just wanted to let you know how much I appreciate your allowing me to stay here. How blessed I feel.

Petra   Oh, how sweet. Oh, thank you.

Mark   So. Good night.

Petra   Well, good night to you too. I hope it's warm enough in here.

Mark   It is. Hey.

Mark *stands and walks over to* **Petra**, *gives her a big hug.*

Petra   Oh.

A few more seconds and the hugs breaks.

Mark   Thank you.

Petra   You're so sweet. Thank you again for the card. It's beautiful.

Mark *goes back to the couch.*

Petra   Good night.

Mark   Good night. And hey. Good for you, Petra.

Petra *(stops, turns)*   What?

Mark   Good for you for quitting stripping.

Scene Six

East Village street. **Mark** *sits with pad, sketching.* **Tan**, *late teens, sees* **Mark**, *watches.* **Tan** *is dressed in old jeans, a long-sleeve T-shirt, and a wool hat.*

Tan   Hey, got a smoke?

Mark *turns.*

Mark   Sorry, I don't smoke.

Tan   No? Wow. 'Cuz you look like you do.

Mark   Sorry.

Mark *turns back to sketching.*

Tan   So why not me?

No response. He moves closer, laughs.

I mean, hey, people in a coffee house, three o'clock, artists, musicians, whatever man. Sitting smoking blah blah blah,

you know? Why draw that? I mean how interesting are *they*?
That's shit, you know? That's like – a bowl of fruit – or my
asshole – would be a better subject.

Mark *smiles politely, continues to sketch.*

Tan *lights a cigarette.* **Mark** *looks.*

Tan   It's my last one. Whatever. You want one?

Mark   I told you.

Tan   Yeah, I know what you told me.

Pause.

'Kay then. Hey, you wanna make a bet?

Mark   A bet.

Tan   I bet you ten bucks I can guess what brand of
underwear you got on.

Mark   Ha, I don't uh.

Tan   Bet it's Calvin Klein.

Beat.

Mark   You're wrong.

Tan   I guess I owe you ten bucks. I don't got it though.
Hey, if you can't guess what kind I'm wearing we'll be even.
Wanna find out?

Mark   No.

Beat. **Tan** *lifts up his shirt, reveals underwear sticking up out of his
jeans.*

Tan   Fruit of the Loom!

Scene Seven

Late lunch. Midtown restaurant.

Petra You know: *What was your major? Oh have I read
anything of yours? Oh my daughter just graduated from law school and
she wrote a legal thriller kind of a John Grisham except a female
version.*

Stephen Brilliant.

Petra Then he asks me what I write. So I think – so I
decide to tell him, who knows, I think, don't judge, okay?
maybe he really cares – you know, I give him the spiel. And
he nods and says: *So why does this job interest you, Patricia?*

Stephen Mmm-hmmm.

Petra So barely an hour ago this is, I still feel two feet tall.
So I say, Look – I'm very blunt – I say, 'I'm looking to work
in a positive, stable environment, where I feel supported,
where my work is appreciated, where there's a sense of
structure,' and I say, and I *say*, 'Because this sense of
structure has been missing from my life.' And he says: *Do you
know Powerpoint? Do you know Excel? Do you know Quark?* No.
No. No. And then! Then: *I actually majored in literature for about
a year as an undergraduate, do you believe that?* And he's laughing;
and I'm *not* laughing. I say Yes. Yes I do believe that.
Because I will not let him know I feel *humiliated*. Because I
will have *dignity* even if – and he says *Well* and they'll be in
touch and on and on and then I'm on the street.

Stephen Well, I'm just – it's enough to make you want to
go back to stripping.

Petra Well, I won't do that. (*Beat.*) I mean, I dressed
appropriately, right?

Stephen Yes! God, I am so far behind in these blurb
reviews, I have to get back.

Petra Right.

Stephen   I mean I have a few more minutes but. Who are these people? Oh – my boss wants to see me at four, who knows what that's about.

Petra   Well, I try to count my blessings but – I can't believe you're eating that burger.

Stephen   I know, it's disgusting, isn't it. I wonder what Mark's doing right now.

Petra   He's a sweetheart, Stephen.

Stephen   Yeah – but this Bible stuff. Whoa, you know.

Petra   It bothers you?

Stephen   No, it's okay, I mean – but – I just feel like we haven't . . . yeah, I mean, of *course* it bothers me – The Lord will provide? But. But I've never been addicted to crack, so. So what do I know. I mean, is he even sleeping with men anymore? I dunno, I just feel like I don't – those missing – oh I dunno, I'm just nervous really about this grant which I should be hearing about but – I wish we had more time, I feel so rushed, it's so hard to connect like this, you know, but: well, what are you doing tonight?

Petra   Oh, I'm seeing some old girlfriends really late – Christmassy thing. After this I'm gonna go to the library before it closes.

Stephen   Well, we'll catch up. Hey, have you seen *Men in Black*?

Petra   No.

Stephen   No. Oh well. I sort of like Will Smith. (*Picking up check.*) Christ, I have to stop this, my bank account is *fucked*.

Petra   Yeah, Will Smith's very charming. They love him in Japan.

Stephen   Yeah, yeah, he's good.

Scene Eight

The apartment. **Tan** *sits on the couch, reads a magazine.* **Mark** *sits at the table with his pad.*

Tan   'How to Get and Keep a Man in Your Bed.' People live like this?

Mark   I don't know.

Tan   'Bulimia's Grip.' 'AIDS and Women: The Unreported Risks.' 'Leonardo DiCaprio Loves His Mom.' Fuck, I'm cuter than Leonardo DiCaprio, he has *no* muscle. *Cosmopolitan* bullshit. I partied with him once, what a *dork*. So a chick lives here. I hope.

He grabs remote, turns on TV. MTV.

Man, this song *bites*. Fucking poseurs. Man, this world is just full of fucking *poseurs*.

Mark   Could you turn that off.

Tan   What?

Mark   I just. I like to control what I. Expose myself to.

Tan   You mean you don't like MTV.

Mark   Well. Sort of.

Tan   'Kay.

He shuts it off. A beat.

So, look, I'm waiting for you to take your dick out and it's been like half an hour and I'm getting a little nervous.

Mark *laughs.*

Tan   I'm not a hustler.

Mark   I should hope you're not. I didn't expect that you were.

Tan   There's only one thing I do for money. I have a specialty. Thing I do I'm famous for is I jerk off on the street. Bare-assed, you know, bare *feet*, not a thing on, just me and my shit. In public, anywhere – it costs a lot because of the risk involved. When a guy tries to pick me up that's what I say, I say I do one thing and it costs three hundred bucks but you've never seen anyone do anything like it and you never will again.

Mark   Sounds dangerous.

Tan   Do you mind if I just jerk off for myself? You can just watch. (*Smiles.*) No charge.

Mark   If you want to do that, you should leave.

Tan   So why would you draw people in a coffee house, artists and shit? That's boring. What are you?

Mark   What am I? I am a filmmaker.

Tan   Oh yeah? You make movies?

Mark   I made one.

Tan   Huh. I know famous people. I told you I partied with Leonardo DiCaprio, dude is *soft*. So um if you like to control what you expose yourself to why'd you invite me over?

Mark   Look. You can leave, I mean. You're free to do whatever you want. I'm not here to. Do anything. To. I just thought. I thought I was being kind. I thought I would show you some kindness.

Tan   Yeah, what's that line, 'I have always depended on the kindness of strangers' or whatever. Cool movie. Ha. Right. Okay. I got. What do I got.

He takes a plastic baggie of pills out from his pocket, lays it on table.

These are not cheap either because these are good, just so you know. I got three Valium – I crush 'em up and snort 'em, you absorb it quicker that way . . . a few Quaaludes. I have these things, basically they're like prescription-strength Motrin, they're not opiate-based so basically they're just for if you have a very bad headache. Got some black tar from a friend out west . . . So.

Mark   I am a recovering drug addict.

Tan   Oh. Wow. Recovering, does that mean . . .

Mark   It means I've been sober for five months.

Tan   So, are you a fag or what?

The door opens. Christmas tree. **Stephen** *enters behind tree.* **Tan** *puts the drugs away.*

Stephen   I got a treee-eee! I got a treee-eee!

He sees.

Oh. Hi.

Mark   That's a beautiful tree.

Stephen   Well, I have to take the wires off, we'll see then. Of course it's too big and there's no space but I figured if we're going to have a beautiful Christmas we need a beautiful tree. Hi, I'm Stephen.

Tan   Hey. Yeah, there's nothing fucking worse than X-mas in New York.

Mark   Stephen, this is Tan.

Stephen   Tan? Tan's a – where did you get that name, it's great.

Tan (*standing*)   Yeah, man, Mark invited me over to take a shower, I thought he was *weird* or something but he's, like, the Pope, so. City's driving me crazy, man! The music – BLAH BLAH BLAH BLAH BLAH BLAH, BLAH BLAH ALL THE WAY – ha! – yeah – you know – and people aren't happy. Couple days they'll be like joining *gyms* and buying the *patch* and shit.

Stephen   Right. Well, only a few more days of that, I guess, so you'll survive. Anyway – I'll just dig up the ornaments and maybe, all of us, we can decorate the tree. I bought some Christmas music too, cheapo cassettes from the Duane Reade, and uhh – alcohol-free egg nog.

He pulls the tapes and the egg nog from the bag and puts them on the kitchen counter.

The ornaments and the lights and stuff are somewhere in my room, so.

He goes into his room. Throughout the following, we see him looking around his cluttered room for decorations.

Tan   He cool?

Mark   Sorry?

Tan   What's he do?

Mark   He writes . . . movie reviews for an online magazine.

Tan   Cool. You two uhh . . . ?

Mark   No.

Tan   Cool. Hey, you know, look, I'm just – I'm not a squatter, okay, I have my own place, I support myself.

Mark   Yes?

Tan   I left home you know because my parents – and school – and me being – all that shit. But I don't want you to think I'm some, like, street-kid poseur 'cuz I'm *not*, some fucking –

Mark   Okay.

Tan   Yeah. So. (*Beat.*) I wanna kiss you, man. You're sweet. You're weird.

Mark   You can't kiss me.

Tan   Why not?

Stephen *enters with a box.*

Stephen   Here we go. Hey, was there anything in the mail for me today?

Mark   Just *The Nation*.

Stephen   Right. Well. Let's take a look!

Stephen *undoes the wires; the tree spreads out.*

Tan   Hey, I think I'll take that shower now.

Mark   All right.

Tan *goes into the bathroom.* **Stephen** *looks at the tree. The shower turns on behind the door.* **Stephen** *turns to* **Mark**.

Stephen   Hey.

Mark   Hi.

Stephen *puts ornaments onto the couch.*

Mark   I feel as though you're upset with me.

Stephen   No – no. This is your home. My home is . . .

Mark   I thought a shower. He was so. Obviously hungry and I was reminded of. I guess he reminded me of – myself and. Clearly this is someone who's been shown no love, and – it seemed like the Christian thing to do.

Stephen   I'm just surprised all your Bible talk didn't scare him off.

Mark   What does that mean?

Stephen   Nothing – I don't mean – anything.

Mark   And I thought, well, maybe I should show some discretion but. But why show discretion because. Because of how we're taught to treat. People. Because how we treat them sometimes – makes them what they are.

Stephen   Absolutely.

Mark   Good.

Pause.

Stephen   So this is the part where you ask about my day.

Mark   I'm sorry. How was your day?

Stephen *starts to put a few decorations on the tree.*

Stephen   They did not like, listen to this, they did not like my blurbs, my blurbs were *rejected*, two of the four because, they said, they used words like brisk and *self-assured* as being qualities my blurbs did not *have*, you know, meaning, these are not *arch* enough, – straight-faced, I'm sitting in the office, I'm nervous actually nervous, and, and have you noticed this trend among women, this trend where they do not *like* homosexual men, I mean I know that's a dangerous generality but she said, These are too *soft*, these lack *punch*, I mean, she might as well have said I don't have the *balls* to write a blurb of *Men in Black*. So. So now I have to rewrite the blurbs and it's like, look, I don't want to go back to temping, which was which was *soul-murder*, which was pure degradation every hour on the hour, and I don't certainly do not want to 'bartend' again and it's getting to the point where it's like – I mean I'm not gonna move where would I *move* Los Angeles? and it's – but what can I do to make money that will not take all my energy and slowly and utterly *kill* me because I have been there before, you know, Huck Finn, 'I've been there before,' and, you know, he's off floating on a raft and happy and won't be civilized and of course he won't go back, he's a bright guy, but then, you know, Mark Twain wrote the book, not Huck Finn –

Apartment buzzer.

Well. Saved by the buzzer just as I was getting incoherent. But I am, I'm enraged, and am I *wrong*, you know, am I *indulgent*, well, I say *No* because that's what they want me to think so I'll shut up and be a good little – (*Pushing intercom button.*) Hello?

Petra (*off*)   Hi, I need help down here.

Stephen   Help?

Petra (*off*)   Come down.

Stephen   Okay.

He lets go of buzzer. Looks at **Mark**.

I hope everything's okay.

Stephen *goes.* **Tan** *emerges from bathroom, not wet, shower running. He's wrapped in a towel.*

Tan   Where'd what's-his-name go?

Mark   Downstairs for a moment. Is something wrong?

Tan   Well, the water pressure was bitching which shocked me so I should have known something was wrong. Um. It just wouldn't get hot. You know. Or even warm. It's ice.

Mark *looks away.*

Tan   Everything okay?

Mark   Yeah.

Tan   Okay. Hey, can I borrow some underwear?

Mark   Sure.

Mark *goes to a bag, gets underwear, hands them to* **Tan**.

Tan   Calvin Klein. Cool. So why'd you invite me here, for real.

Mark   I've told you. (*Beat.*) I bought some pie this morning. Would you like a piece?

Tan   Pie?

Mark   Apple pie.

Tan   Whatever.

Tan *goes back into the bathroom. Shower cuts off. Door opens. A tree.*

Stephen   Surprise!

They enter, with the tree, which is smaller than the first.

Petra   I had no idea. Ridiculous, can you believe it?

Stephen   It's a great New York story.

Petra   Two trees we have.

Stephen   I told Petra this'd be our affirmative action tree – we'll put Kwanzaa and Hanukkah ornaments on it.

Petra   Don't forget Solstice, people are getting into this whole Solstice thing.

Stephen *puts the tree in an opposite corner, sets it against the wall.*

Petra   I wanted to cheer myself up because of this interview, so I bought it.

Mark   Petra, do you want a piece of pie?

Petra   Pie?

Mark   Apple p— that's right, the –

Petra *(laughs)*   – no carbs.

Mark   How about it, Stephen. Let's have some pie.

Stephen   Well – all right.

Petra   Oh, the best part I didn't tell you, the best part was how the guy kept telling me how skinny I was, at the interview, during, and finally he goes and comes back with a bagel. He says, You're going to eat this, and then I had to explain the whole no-carb thing to him.

Stephen   This no-carb thing sounds like a cult.

Tan *comes out of the bathroom, fully dressed.*

Tan   Hey.

Stephen   Hey, Tan. We have two trees to decorate now. You wanna help?

Tan   I actually have a thing to go to, so, you know how it is.

Mark   You're leaving?

Stephen   Tan, this is Petra, Petra, Tan.

Petra   Hello.

Tan   Hey. Yeah, so. Hey, thanks for the underwear.

Mark   You're welcome.

Tan   Yeah . . . Fuck, I'm looking for a jacket, I'm realizing I don't have one! Stupid!

Stephen   Oh, you should have a coat.

Tan   Whatever, global warming, El Niño, I'm okay.

Stephen   I'm sure I have a coat you can take.

Tan   I don't know, will it match my sensibility? Ha.

Stephen   Well . . .

Petra   I have a man's hat you're welcome to take.

Tan   Got a hat.

Takes it from his pocket, throws it on. **Stephen** *grabs long gray overcoat from closet.*

Stephen   Here, I don't wear this.

Tan   Really?

He takes it, puts it on.

Cool, I look like a dirty old man, like a flasher or somebody.

He 'flashes' and laughs.

Okay, merry X-mas, joy on earth, peace to the world, all that shit. ('*Bye.*') Bah!

Stephen   Bye.

Mark   Bye, Tan.

He goes. A moment.

Petra   So . . . who was that?

Stephen   Friend of Mark's. He was struck by the Christmas spirit and offered a streetboy a place to shower. He seems like a nice kid.

Mark   He is.

Stephen   That's sad.

Mark   He said the water didn't get hot.

Stephen   The shower? Really?

Stephen *goes into the bathroom. Shower cuts on.* **Mark** *goes, off.*

Petra   How was your day, Mark?

Mark (*off*)   I did a sketch today. How was your day?

Petra   I suppose it could have been worse.

Mark (*off*)   That's a good attitude to have.

Stephen *returns.*

Stephen   Hot water's fine.

Mark *returns with a piece of pie on a plate and a fork.*

Mark   Huh.

Stephen   Maybe he didn't know how to turn it on or something.

Mark (*laughs*)   Well, I'm sure that wasn't it, it's a knob.

Stephen   Well – okay. Well, maybe you're right. Maybe he didn't want to take a shower, how's that. So – tonight we decorate? Petra?

Petra   Oh, remember tonight I'm going out with some old girlfriends? And I have to find some time to read tonight, I'm behind in my reading.

Stephen   Okay. Well, we'll find a time we can all do it. Mark, maybe we'll go to a movie. I was telling Mark they rejected my blurbs today.

Petra   Oh, really?

Stephen   Yeah, I don't want to talk about it.

Petra   Well, I am going to take a little nap, I think.

Stephen   Okay.

Petra *goes.*

Stephen   So. Movie.

Mark   Actually, you know. This will sound – odd, but. I don't go to movies anymore.

Stephen   Oh.

Mark   It just. I like to control what I. Expose myself to.

Stephen   Well, not every movie is directed by Quentin Tarantino.

Mark   I know that. Here.

Hands **Stephen** *a plate of pie, with fork, goes off.*

Mark (*off*)   Yeah, I think I'll just read and take a shower and get to bed early tonight.

Stephen *goes to couch, sits.*

Stephen   Okay. Well. Well, maybe it's the perfect time to finish my Christmas shopping. I just figured out what I'm going to get you.

Mark *returns with a bottle of water.*

Stephen   Well, maybe tonight after I shop we'll just hang out and talk, we can talk –

Stephen *takes a bite of pie.* **Mark** *goes to the couch, sits.*

Mark   I'll be asleep when you get back most likely.

Stephen (*chewing*)   Oh, right. Where's your piece?

Mark   I'm not having one.

Stephen   – Oh.

Mark *smiles. As does* **Stephen**. **Mark** *takes a sip of water.*
Stephen *swallows his bite of pie.*

Scene Nine

Strip club. **Petra** *with the same* **Man** *as before.*

Petra   Before he died, then, you actually knew him.

Man   I used to go to this diner all the time he worked at,
you know, by where I live, the show was going up, we were
all real excited for him – he was just our waiter, at the time.

Petra   Wow.

Man   Do you like it? You've seen it?

Petra   I have.

Man   You said you lived in the East Village, so I –

Petra   No, I understand.

Man   I mean, you're not – perhaps I'm being dumb, or
presumptuous, I mean, what do I know? . . .

Petra   You're not being dumb.

Man   But you don't like the show, or? The critics, they
liked it, people, people seem to – standing ovation the night
I saw it – Pulitzer Prize. So I'm interested in why, if – isn't
that – East Village – but – why don't you talk?

Petra   Look – thirteen-year-old kids, fat girls, gay boys,
they love it, so. I don't, truly, I don't think about it. No. If I
did think about it I would get angry because. Because it's
another example of. It's – *condescending*.

Man   How is that?

Petra   Because. Because I work hard and. I work to try to
be an *artist* – which, it's an embarrassment to even use that
word –

Man   Why?

Petra   Listen – I read. I work hard. And what the show says to me is – is am I indecent, or, or am I 'selling out' or am I *inauthentic* because I want, I want money or, or an apartment which is even just *decent*? I mean, when do any of those characters read? What are they doing with all their time, I don't – and we *celebrate* these people, and don't get me wrong, everyone is *valuable*, but, but *what* are we celebrating?

Man   Life. The artistic life. Refusal to compromise. Right?

Petra   Wanna know who lives in the East Village? A lot of the actors in the show, that's who. Those characters, it's like Peter Pan Neverland, refusal to grow up, join the real – I know it's a *musical* but it avoids asking any real, I mean, *genuine* questions and instead makes – makes a mockery of – my roommate said this and I agree – makes a *spectacle* of AIDS, gays, lesbians, blacks – it – *commodifies* actual – and tell me these people who are in it and who directed it have no idea how they're mocking themselves and their – their own *choices* – oh whatever.

Man   No, no, please, this is! – You're . . . how can I say this . . . threatened then. By these characters.

Petra   Well. What I was going to say was. I'm not used to having to think too hard when I'm here.

Man   Change the subject then. I want to hear one of your poems.

Petra   Oh come on.

Man   Why are you embarrassed? My goodness, the fact that you write poems – is fascinating to me! Would you tell me one?

Petra   I, they're written down, so.

Man   See, you are just – who you are – comes through and is – fascinating! So. So I know this isn't – I'm not stupid –

He takes out his wallet.

I'm under no –

He puts money on the table.

There. For a poem. For one poem.

Petra   I'll talk to you but. No.

Man   Okay. Okay. We talk. Here: I just saw this movie? *Boogie Nights?* What did you think of it?

Petra   All those movies, *Trainspotting, Boogie Nights,* I – I can't.

Man   Can't . . . ? You don't . . . obviously don't –

Petra   It's immoral because – I live in *this world* and – they – they romanticize – and *ignore* – what – they leave out of this experience, this, being alive – and I think: Is this what I must include? To be *valued?* Rewarded? *Depravity?* To be seen must I write what is more or less – more or less *pornography*, something that *titillates* with violence and sex? Or else – *My Best Friend's Wedding* and *The Celestine Prophecy?* Do you see?

Man   I come here, you know.

Petra   You . . . ?

Man   You say: I live in this world. And I am interested in your opinions. I ask you about these plays and movies, which *I* see, which *you* see . . .

Petra   *(her expression reads 'I don't understand what you meant by "I come here"')*   You come here?

Man   Here. How can I . . . ?

Petra   Oh – it just gets me so angry. Drugs – drugs are not – violence, real violence, life, *life* – the poor, criminals, it is not – we romanticize it – it is like – a drug – like – the trauma, the trauma of actually seeing this world is such that we create fantasies, we reward those who create *fantasies*

because God forbid we look at – reality – at *ourselves* – there
are people in this country, *other people* who are fascinating
and, and *troubled* – and yet – where are they? – and New
York and Los Angeles constantly dump this – shit this shit
into this country and people will – eat it because they're
hungry – these crumbs – and I don't – I'm not judging those
who watch or, or *read* this stuff – I watch it too sometimes –
but I blame those who – look – I am trying to *transcend* – but
there are pressures which prevent me – many *pressures* and –
I mean you say: you say, I come here. I say: I work here.

Man   I come here for fantasy. Is what I was going to say.
And what is so wrong with fantasy? If that's what we need to
live. Because. Don't we all have fantasies?

Petra   But there's a moral . . . in terms of art . . .

She stops.

I'm sorry.

Man   Here's the deal. I want you to show me your life.
Because it is so distant from my life. This is why I go to
movies, and plays. And come here. And so I know, I am
aware that perhaps you will find this – distasteful. Or
immoral even. But you would get to see my life. Which you,
you could not fathom. Where I work. The conversations I
have. I am asking for – some time – dinner, dates, you will
take me to coffee where you have coffee, I will take you to
dinner where I have dinner. I don't – I'm a gentle man –
and I am a – frightened man – and curious – and I don't – I
know without money I am nothing to you. I am a very rich
person, and I have herpes so I don't really have sex
anymore.

Pause.

Petra   Let me ask you this. Why if you are interested in
getting to know somebody, in intimacy, why would you
come here? To a pornographic place?

Man   You're right. But I'll pay you not to come here. To accompany me as though –

Petra   But why – in the first place – you're – you have money – you're – nice – and attractive –

Man   Oh, come now. You tell me, how else might I have met you. In a club? Come up to you in some club in Tribeca, 'Hey, how are you?'

Petra   But – I'm not talking about just *me* –

Man   I am. I find *you* fascinating. I don't find my secretary fascinating, I'm sorry.

Pause.

Petra   I work here, this is my job, I don't go home as this person, I –

Man   Here.

He takes out a hundred-dollar bill and writes on it.

Now you can call me and. Call me and just. Talk to me about your life. And then. We can get together and have dinner and coffee a couple of times and I will pay you for your time. (*Rising.*) Take care, Petra.

He goes. She takes the hundred dollars.

Act Two

Scene One

Christmas Eve day. An apartment. **Darren** *is sitting on a sofa, flipping through some channels.* **Stephen** *is pouring and steeping tea. A lava lamp on a nightstand, red globs in yellow water.* **Darren** *has a slight, ambiguous, Britishy-sounding accent.*

Darren   I'm glad you called. I didn't know why you didn't call.

Stephen   Oh, yeah. No I really liked you, I just, I was so overwhelmed and I've *been* so overwhelmed but lately I've just been feeling such a need to *connect*, things have been so – it's probably just the holidays, but. You know, God, these tea cups are gorgeous! I mean, that's kind of a weird thing to say, but. Do you, sugar, or? Darren?

Darren   Oh, yeah, just – this show. Yeah, an embarrassing amount of sugar. Yeah, that set was a thousand dollars, the cups and the plates and stuff.

Stephen   *What?*

Darren   Oh, that's right, you don't know – I sold a screenplay.

Stephen   Oh, you did?

Darren   Yeah, *and* made a deal to co-produce the sound-track. Three hundred thousand dollars against seven hundred.

Stephen   Oh my God! Well, that's extraordinary! Well – my God!

Darren   Yeah, like four spoonfuls.

Stephen   Okay. Well, what's the screenplay about?

Darren   Oh, you know, romantic comedy, East Villagers meeting cute, you know, stockbroker guy runs into squatter girl at ATM, blah blah blah the end.

Stephen   Well, congratulations!

Darren   Are you still working on that play?

Stephen   Yeah, I am.

Darren   What's it about again?

Stephen   This incredible thing that happened in my hometown, this amazingly beautiful –

Darren   Where are you from again?

Stephen   Darien, Connecticut? Kind of, kind of upper-middle-class suburb, about an hour away.

Stephen *comes to the couch with the tea.*

Darren   So what are you doing for Christmas Eve tonight?

Stephen   Oh, um –

Darren   I have to make the rounds at these endless horrible parties. Then I have to go out to la-la land on the 26th, so it's kind of a truncated holiday.

Stephen   Right. Yeah, I'm not going home to my family, first time actually, that would just be self-loathing, and I have two friends in town so –

Darren   Do you like my lava lamp? I can't make up my mind about it.

Stephen   Oh – I don't like them in general. I always, I always thought they kind of looked like, I don't know, an abortion or something.

Darren   Really?

Stephen   Yeah.

Darren   That's kind of witty.

Stephen   Oh?

Darren   There's *nothing* on.

Stephen   So how's Maria?

Darren   Maria?

Stephen   What was her name? Marla?

Darren   Magda, my friend Magda. Hey. I have something you'll like.

He puts in a tape.

Watch this.

He sits back on the couch.

Stephen   God! it's so *nice* to have a day off. Oh. Oh God.

Darren   This is that homemade porno –

Stephen   Oh.

Darren   They *totally* wanted it released, I mean gimme a break – I have a friend who gets all these, he got the, remember the Rob Lowe tape? but that's pretty boring. This is *hot*. Look at how big Tommy Lee's dick is. That's a fucking beautiful cock, you have to admit.

Stephen   Wow, it's really them. Pamela Anderson. Wow.

Darren *puts his hand in his pants, starts moving it around.*

Stephen   Oh. Oh God you know. Maybe. I feel – I hope I didn't imply by just – calling up and coming over – that I wanted to –

Darren *unzips his fly, reaches in that way.*

Stephen   You know, I think I'm gonna go.

Darren   Aw, come on.

Stephen   Yeah, I don't . . . I don't know. Yeah, I think I'm gonna go.

Darren   Hey, I'll stop the tape. No big deal.

Stephen   You know it's – I didn't, I just didn't expect you know – I hope I'm not – I just, I just –

Darren   Do you have an erection?

Stephen   What?

Darren   I'm asking if you have a hard-on. We'll just beat off.

Stephen   Well, I mean –

Darren   If you're not gonna answer me –

Darren *reaches for* **Stephen***'s crotch.* **Stephen** *spills his tea.*

Stephen   Oh –

Darren   Ow! – You didn't have to spill the tea, Stephen – fuck! Ouch.

Stephen   I didn't mean to – my unconscious talking I guess.

Darren   Well, why don't you leave before your unconscious breaks my VCR or my lava lamp.

Stephen   Good idea. Hah. Well, my therapist will love hearing about this.

Darren   Okay.

Stephen   My jacket.

He gets his jacket, puts it on. **Darren** *goes off, into the bathroom. Water running.*

Stephen   You know, I was just, just hoping to talk, you know, about, just. Sorry. Okay. Well, hey, have a good Christmas.

Darren (*off*)   You too.

Stephen *hesitates. Touches his crotch, rubs. He looks off to the bathroom, looks quickly to the TV.*

Darren   Hello?

Stephen   Yeah, no, I'm going – I just – I'll call you when – I mean I like you I feel – it's not that I don't want to, to – I just –

Darren (*off*)   Okay, gotcha. Take care!

Stephen   You too!

Stephen *goes*.

Scene Two

A restaurant, fancy, conservative. Classical piano, far-off.

Man   So what are you doing after dinner. How are you spending your Christmas Eve?

Petra   Well, my two roommates are . . . we're exchanging gifts. And it's been a nightmare.

Man   What's going on?

Petra   Basically, my roommate Stephen's ex-lover, his name is Mark, had this big deal in Hollywood, started filming this movie, started doing a lot of drugs, then towards the end of it I guess basically had a nervous breakdown – so he went into rehab and became – found God more or less. And he's become friends with this street kid who's obviously unhealthy and on drugs and – he's ignoring Stephen, so. And this is very hard for Stephen to understand. So basically.

Man   Wow.

Petra   What?

Man   Fascinating. People. Their *lives*. My God.

Petra   What are *you* doing tonight?

Man   Nothing. Watch TV. Tomorrow I'm gonna drive to Connecticut and see my folks. (*Beat.*) What do you think of this restaurant?

Petra   It's lovely. I'm so excited for my monkfish.

Man   The monkfish, I've had it before. It's good.

Petra   I can't wait.

Man   Can I ask you a question?

Petra   Yes.

Man   And by the way, you look beautiful tonight. Stunning.

Petra   Thank you.

Man   Do your roommates tell you you're beautiful?

Petra   No.

Man   Well, they should.

Petra   You're sweet.

Man   Why do you strip? (*Beat.*) Why do you keep – when obviously you don't have to?

Petra   Oh, is that obvious?

Man   Is it material? Do you get good material?

Petra   God, no.

Man   So it's really just. The money.

Petra   Well . . .

Man   New York City's so expensive.

Petra   Well, yes, but it's. Where. I feel I have to be.

Man   It's a big country.

Petra   But – here – the arts – that industry is . . . here. And I grew up here, to leave . . .

Man   I see these guys at the club. You put yourself through a lot of misery.

Petra   There's a lot – really – that I enjoy about dancing.
A lot that I find fulfilling but. You know, office work is no
less demeaning. And yes, I do believe I learn, or see, have
access to particular men, there's a rare intimacy about the
setting . . .

Man   But it must make you crazy.

Petra   Crazy.

Man   You can tell me if I'm wrong.

Petra   I . . . enjoy it. Dancing I. It makes me feel good.

Man   Good how?

Petra   It makes me feel special.

Pause.

Man   I write poems sometimes, you know. (*Beat.*) Does
that surprise you?

Petra   No.

Man   You want to be a writer, but I – well – I just dabble,
nothing serious, just for me. See, generally I run away. I go
to a spa. I see a movie. Take a trip. That's what I do. But
you. You walk head-first into it – your pain – every day.
You have to, else you wouldn't be a writer.

Petra   No.

Man   No?

Petra   No, because pain – and consciousness – both are
difficult but – I should hope there's a difference between the
two. I think I am *conscious*. But pain – I don't want my pain
any more than you want yours.

Man   See, that's what I – I mean, what *makes* you an
artist? What happened to make you – I know how I got into
investment banking, it's a pretty simple story. But you. This
person you are, this *life*, what made you – how did it
happen?

Petra   Okay. Okay. I'm a freshman in college. A dorm, like a prison, falling apart, roaches, like rats in a lab we are, okay? My roommate is – Dominican or something – and one night she makes this big greasy pot of fish, in this very greasy yellow sauce, and she leaves it simmering on the stove. She goes out to meet her boyfriend. I go into the kitchen. I open the pot. Me. And it looks like sewage. A huge – ridiculous this pot is. And I take out a spoon and think: I'll try this. And I do. I take another bite. Another. And I know, I am a rational being, I know she's cooked this for her boyfriend, they'll be back soon: the whole pot. All of it. And I run into the bathroom and I sit there I'm numb I put my hand into my mouth, okay? And I'm covered there in – fish – covered – I look – a ghoul – green, literally – and I'm thinking: *What?* Because I know enough to know this is not normal or healthy in any way and I want to know: *Why?* Why would I have done this: why do I feel this way? What in the world – literally, what in the world in which I find myself living, what at this point in history, what could make a person feel this unbearable sadness and think these terrible thoughts? These thoughts: *I will never be loved. I cannot live in this world.* You see? Because – because my roommate is going to come home and say Where is the fish and the only answer is Petra ate it. Petra ate the fish. And how can I go on? How can I go on without – and I know – that there are people who do not ask this question – because to know – is too much. Because society does not *afford* them the opportunity to know, and. Because they are in a constant state of *desire* and desire, *want*, inhibits consciousness. To become conscious you must stifle yourself, resist your impulses. Not that I had this language then. But I knew; I decided. I decided next time I would not eat the fish. No matter what. No matter what pain that caused me I would put the fork down and place the lid on the pot and.

Pause.

Man   What's your name?

Petra   My name is Petra.

Man   What's your real name?

Petra   My name is Petra.

Pause.

Man   Two years ago I bought my wife a necklace. For
Christmas. Okay. She opened it up – she didn't like it. And
I said, Well, it's okay, take it back. But I felt . . . angry. I felt
. . . sick. And then she stopped sleeping with me. Why? I
didn't know. And then I was on a trip. I met a woman in a
bar. And I had told myself many times that I would never,
but I was angry at my wife. I. Hated her. Despised – and so,
and so I had sex with this woman from the bar. So what
you're saying is . . .

Petra   Do you see? My story illustrates my awakening to
consciousness; yours does not. This is the difference – what I
was trying to say the other night – this is the difference
between art and pornography as well. Art can be ugly and
painful and full of disgusting things; but unlike pornography
it is conscious of this.

Man   Conscious or not, it's still horrible. Horrible. Look at
. . . Woody Allen – the ways people behave – despite what
they know – I mean, when did he decide, you know, to? I'm
not an intellectual man. I don't have words. Thank you,
Petra. Thank you for – you.

Pause.

Are you still in pain?

Petra   – No.

Man   I can't say I believe you, Petra.

Petra   No. No. I have beauty in my life. I have art, I have
friends –

Man   That's not what I asked.

They look at each other.

I can't wait for the food. This is the best food.

He sips from a glass of wine.

Scene Three

Apartment, that night. **Stephen** *arrives, entering with a bag.* **Mark***'s on the phone, quickly hangs up.*

Stephen   Hey, sweets!

Mark   Hi.

Stephen   Merry Christmas Eve. How are you?

Mark   I'm fine. How are you?

Stephen   Ugh shopping is *done*!

Mark   Good day?

Stephen   Great day! You?

Mark   Okay.

Stephen   How's Tan?

Mark   He hasn't come by.

Stephen   Oh? I hope he's all right.

Mark   Me too.

Stephen   So are you all ready for Christmas Eve?

Mark   Yes.

Stephen   Are you going to church?

Mark   Tomorrow morning.

Stephen   Oh, maybe I can go with you.

Mark   I don't think that's appropriate.

Stephen   Oh?

Mark   My faith is very special to me. I take it very seriously.

Stephen   Well – I'm not going to sit there making pedophile jokes about the priest.

Mark   I'm sorry. You understand.

Stephen   Well. Okay, whatever you need. I bumped into Petra at the deli, she'll be here in a couple of minutes.

He goes into his room, takes stuff out of the bags.

So were you on the phone with Hollywood?

Mark   When?

Stephen   When I came in. You were on the phone.

Mark   No, I was thinking of calling someone.

Stephen   Oh. Hey, did you get the mail?

Mark   Yeah, you didn't get anything.

Stephen   Fuck.

Mark   I got something.

Stephen   Yeah?

Mark   They sent me the cut of the movie.

Stephen *re-enters the living room. Sees the large envelope atop the VCR.*

Stephen   The – your movie?

Mark   I need to make a decision by – it's going to be at Sundance – so they need to know. If I want. My name on it. I haven't – watched it yet.

Stephen   Wow . . . well, I'm sure that's going to be difficult for you.

Mark   What do you care about Tan?

Beat.

Stephen   Excuse me?

Mark   When you came in. 'How's Tan?'

Stephen   Are we all right here?

Mark   I mean just let me live my life don't. Judge me all the time.

Stephen   O-kay . . . is there . . . something you'd like to talk about?

Mark   How's Tan, Who were you on the phone with, I mean. Just – no – exactly – there is nothing about all this I'd like to talk to you about as long as you're *judging* me –

Stephen   All right, wait a second –

Mark   Your rage is so transparent and it's just toxic, you know, it's poisoning this whole –

Stephen   Rage?

Mark   Yes, rage, at me, yes. I'm sorry we're not having sex, I'm sorry this is so upsetting to you.

Stephen   *Mark?*

Mark   'How's Tan?'

Stephen   Okay, okay, I'm not going to yell and, and also it's Christmas Eve, but what I will say, what I will say is that you're, you're really – hurting my feelings here. Okay? So just – so just be a human being here for a second and let's go back to –

Mark   *What?*

Stephen   What? What?

Mark   What, I don't know how to be a human being now?

Stephen   That's not what I said.

Mark   What did you say then?

Stephen   Okay, let's take deep breaths –

Mark   Can you SHUT UP for a second? you're always fucking TALKING.

Stephen   Shut – Mark – what – I ask how you are, I ask about your life – you know if anyone should be angry here – Jesus Fucking Christ! –

Mark   Oh, thank you.

Stephen   Oh, *oh*, excuse me for taking the fucking Lord's name in vain, I'm sorry I'm not SPIRITUAL like you taking you know fucking becoming intimate with a fucking STREET KID hustler drug dealer whatever and you can't, you can't even fucking find ten MINUTES to talk to me –

Mark   Stop yelling! –

Stephen   Stop – no! – you don't, you don't ask to even read what I'm working on, you sit here all day, *my* house, you invite this *kid* –

Mark   So you're jealous, because you think, you have some *idea* –

Stephen   Well, I'm sorry if I'm a little fucking cynical, I mean, where's, how are you being a good Christian all this religious BULLSHIT, I mean, go fucking pass out food to smelly ugly homeless men, don't give me this Christian shit about – being –

Mark   Stop yelling!

Stephen   – no, go deliver food to people dying of AIDS, go, fuck you –

Mark   STOP YELLING!

Pause. **Mark** *beginning to cry.*

Stephen   Oh – come on – don't – don't – why are you – don't cry –

Mark   You know I was – I was – away for a long time I wasn't in the world and – I'm *adjusting* you know and it's not – I'm doing the best I – it's hard and you could show some – compassion –

Stephen   Come on, don't cry –

Mark   – because – I just wanted – a safe space and – you fucking accuse me of – all this judging, all this – let he who is without sin cast the first – you know? – I never said I was – perfect and I'm sorry if I'm not who – you wanted – me – to be – anymore –

Stephen   No, that's not – come on, don't cry. That's not it. I'm sorry, I shouldn't have – yelled I.

Mark *breaks down.* **Stephen** *puts his arm around him.*

Stephen   I just – if you're in pain I want to – it's – shhhh, come on. Shhh. It's okay. Shhh.

Mark   I have to go to the bathroom.

Mark *gets up, goes to the bathroom off. Door opens.* **Petra**. **Stephen** *picks up the phone, pushes a button.*

Petra   Hey!

Stephen   Hi.

Petra   Who are you talking to?

Stephen   Shhhh.

Stephen *listens. Then gasps.*

Petra   What?

Stephen *hangs up.*

Petra   Is Mark home?

Toilet flushes. **Mark** *enters, not crying.*

Petra   Hey, sweetie!

Mark   Hey, Pet.

Mark *goes over to* **Petra**, *gives her a big hug and a kiss.*

Petra   Okay, boys. Are you ready for something?

Stephen   Uh-oh.

Petra   Look what I *bought* myself for Christmas – can you guess?

Stephen   What is it?

Petra   Okay, get ready . . .

She opens her bag and removes: a bagel. She laughs hysterically.
Stephen *and* **Mark** *laugh with her.*

Scene Four

Apartment. Trees are decorated. Some presents and wrapping paper scattered. Laughter. Christmas music playing softly. **Petra** *has her arm around* **Mark**. **Stephen** *sits across from them. Occasionally* **Petra** *runs her hand through* **Mark**'s *hair. The large envelope is still atop the TV.*

Petra   No, I have another one. Even worse.

Stephen   Okay, wait, neither of you knows this one. I am at an audition for a play, this is back like three years ago, and it was a serious play, you know, really heady stuff, and I'm standing outside the room waiting, and we were to wait in this hallway while the auditions were going on, and I'm standing outside the room waiting, whatever, and I hear the actor giving his reading, of the sides. And I got a little startled and nervous because it was a very good reading, really unique and unorthodox but honest and risky, and suddenly my reading seemed so conventional. So he leaves, and he's this striking blond man, glowing eyes, very, that kind of ethereal beauty – and I say hey and he says hey and he goes down the stairs, and I'm waiting: I can hear the casting directors talking – the door to the room is made of this really cheap wood, it's like, cork or something, right? So

I hear this older man's voice, middle-aged, and I hear him say, 'My God, I could fuck that boy a thousand ways to Sunday. My *God*.' You know. And this woman laughs and says, 'He is *ohhhh*,' and I hear the man say, 'And he is *stacked* beneath those clothes, I can tell.' And I hear someone else laugh. And, and then I hear footsteps, the door opens for me, and I go in, and there they are: poker-faced. And I say hi, and I meet the reader, some effeminate twenty-three-year-old, the third person I heard laughing. And I do my reading, very good, blah blah blah, good job, nice to see you, Stephen. But all I'm thinking, I'm leaving and I'm thinking, and I couldn't stay to listen to what they said obviously, there's another actor there now, but I'm walking down the stairs onto horrible West 42nd Street and it's cold and the only thought in my mind is: Did he want to fuck me a thousand ways to Sunday? Nothing about my audition, my reading, my talent, my choices, no, all I could think was: Did he wonder what I looked like under my clothes? And I felt soft and miserable. And went to the gym. For about a week. But. Like. I mean – it was all I cared about, would that fat fifty-year-old jerk off to my headshot that night?

Petra   Because what can you do in that situation? You want the role! It's a good play so how do you not become, in some way, the person they want you to be? You have to be a Zen Master not to want him to masturbate onto your headshot!

Mark   How we treat people – sometimes makes them what they are.

Stephen   God – you know? Who are these people? How do they sleep at night? Shame on them! Oh!

Petra   People, my God. What about you, sweetie? You have any horror stories? My God, this is such a catharsis for me, it's such a *release* hearing all this stuff.

Mark   Um. Well. Yeah, I.

Petra   Oh yeah? Good.

Mark   When I was um. Making my film, about two weeks
before my, whatever, my, you know . . . okay: I'm just
gonna try to – tell this. Okay. Deep breath, wow. Okay. So.
We all went out after the shoot and basically started off by
getting drunk before we moved on, you know, to everything
else. And. I sat there with my actors and. This one, Adam,
said to the group, said. *Mark fucks like a Calvin Klein ad.* Out
of. The blue and. Adam had a small role, and the actors
didn't know him too well but he was my friend so. He'd
come out with us. We'd been talking about how many
people we'd. Slept with. Was the topic of conversation and.
I'd found myself *inflating.* Because I was embarrassed at how,
comparatively, how *few.* Anyway. The actors look at him
and. I say. What can I say? *That was a long time ago.* Not even
a year, Adam says. And the actors start *laughing.* Well. *What
do you mean by that?* And Adam says. *I mean he has this vacant
stare which never changes.* And I. Smile. And I say. *Adam, you
never open your eyes during sex so how would you know.* And.

He starts to cry a little. **Petra** *grabs his hand.*

Mark   It was just then that I. I realized I. Well. So I
laughed. We all laughed and. That night another actor
came to my room at the hotel we. In West Hollywood, a
nice, the Mondrian, we were there for two nights while we
were filming in LA. And this actor came in and. Went in
and turned on the shower and said. We're gonna take a
shower and fuck and I have some Percosets for later my
mom she went just went to the dentist and. And. I did
because.

He stops the story. And stops crying. And laughs. And then silence.

Because, you know. Because I thought . . .

He waves his hand, as if to signal that he won't go on. **Stephen**
grabs a small wrapped flat gift.

Stephen   Here, here, last one.

Petra   Ooooh.

Stephen   For you, Mark.

Mark   You got me another gift? Wow.

Stephen   Well, it's a little self-serving because it's for both of us, but –

He hands **Mark** *a small envelope.* **Mark** *opens it, takes out two tickets.*

Mark   Oh, wow.

Stephen   It's supposed to be really good, it was a hit in London or whatever, so, and it's in previews now, and I thought. We used to have so much fun going to plays together, that used to be our thing, so. I thought it would be nice. And we could go eat after at Leshko's like we did when we had no money. And the only difference would be that we didn't have to usher to get in, or get TKTS or whatever.

Mark   Great.

Stephen   Yeah, so. Hey. Three minutes to Christmas! Eleven fifty-seven . . . now!

Mark   Thank you. It's on New Year's Eve.

Stephen   Yes. There's this, someone was telling me about some culture which believes in spending New Year's Eve in a ritualized, like, in this way where everything you do you do in hopes that your year will follow in that fashion. So if you want a year of clarity, you spend the evening cleaning your home – you make it symbolic and – so I just thought going to a play, karma-wise, might be a really nice, low-key way –

The buzzer buzzes.

Huh?

Petra   Who in God's name?

Stephen *answers with intercom.*

Stephen   Hello?

Tan (*off/through intercom*)   Hey uhh – Mark?

Stephen *looks to* **Mark**.

Tan   Mark, come down! It's Tan!

Mark *stands*.

Mark   I suppose I should . . . go see him for a minute . . .
I guess.

Stephen   Oh, okay.

Mark *grabs his coat and his sketchpad*.

Petra   I hope he's all right.

Mark   I'll be back.

Mark *goes to the door, gets his coat*. **Petra** *starts collecting
wrapping paper*. **Stephen** *goes to* **Mark**.

Stephen   Hey, are you going to be all right?

Mark   Yeah.

Stephen   I'm sorry about earlier.

Mark   It's okay.

Stephen   Anything you need, you know.

Mark   I know.

Stephen   If you're out just call – if you want to talk when
you get back – just knock on my door.

Mark   Thanks a lot. Bye.

Stephen   See you later.

Mark *exits, door slams*.

Petra   That kid is bad news, I hope he knows what he's
doing.

Stephen   Well, listen to this. We got into a little tiff before
you got home – and he – you won't believe this – and I
grabbed the phone because he had been on it when I came

home, and I just hit the redial, and wouldn't you know – no, guess. Guess who he's talking to.

Petra   Ethan Hawke, how the hell do I know.

Stephen   Phone sex.

Petra   Oh.

Stephen   He's. A fucking mess is what he is. He said he's – whatever. Merry Fucking Christmas, Mark. I mean, what can I do?

Petra   Well . . . you can –

Stephen   It's not fair. He can't be honest with me? I love him. I love him and I've done nothing except try to help him. This Bible shit.

Petra   Maybe that's what he needs, Stephen.

Stephen   These stupid recovery programs!

Petra   Why are they stupid?

Stephen   Because they turn people into – all that *shit* about 'That was some other person who was addicted, that was not me' and 'God give me the strength'. So he can't talk to me but he can call phone sex, FUCK him!

Petra   He's a recovering drug addict. He must be –

Stephen   What, is this another I'm OK You're OK no, no, I am *fine* and *he* is fucked up, so, so I'm being judgmental, well, so *fine*, I think I'm allowed I think that's IN FACT I think it's *important*.

Petra   Okay, calm down. I think you should try to understand that –

Stephen   And, and he buys me a BIBLE for Christmas! A Bible! Whooo!

Petra   It's just his way of telling you who he is now. He's sharing –

Stephen – yeah –

Petra   Try to be selfless, take a step back and you'll see –

Stephen   Selfless? What, am I a therapist? No, I – I let him – I love him – I LOVE HIM – and he's – who the fuck knows what he's doing – he could be – you know? –

Petra   I'm not on his side, I'm just trying –

Stephen   Oh no, well, what's with, with all this, this hands all over him always hugging him, what the hell is that?

Petra   I don't understand.

Stephen   I mean, there you are, I mean, what about me? Who's holding my hand? Who's hugging me? And where's my two-million-dollar three-picture deal?

Petra   I think you have to ask yourself why you're so upset, Stephen.

Stephen   Because I am, and I'm allowed to be fucking upset, so – so fuck you too!

Stephen *picks up some wrapping paper, puts it into the garbage, goes to his room, shuts the door. Climbs into bed. Petra looks around. She takes a small gift and unwraps it. It's her bagel. She sits on the couch and takes a bite of it.*

Scene Five

A luxurious bathroom. A huge, white circular bathtub; gray mottled walls. Gleaming chrome fixtures. Mirrors. A bathroom at the Royalton Hotel.

Tan   It's cool, isn't it.

Mark   It's really beautiful. So peaceful. Clean.

Tan   I swear to God. He books the room an extra night and leaves, lets me have it. Like once a month. Isn't that weird?

Mark   And all he leaves is dirty underwear?

Tan   He leaves them under the bed. And they're smeared
– you know, cum, shit, piss. You know. But – I tell him I
jerk off onto them and then I mail them back to him. He
leaves the envelope, already stamped and shit. But I don't
jerk off onto them, and he can't tell the difference.

Mark   Sick.

Tan   So I just come and take a bath. Sometimes I order
porno. They have that Simon Rex jerk-off tape, *Young Hard
and Solo 2*.

Mark   Do they?

Tan   And I order a Black Angus. Mmmmmm.

Mark   Wow.

Tan   We can eat whatever. Just charge it to the bill. Guy's
loaded. I met him by jerking off for him. And he always
leaves a couple hundreds hid somewhere. In the room, you
know. He draws little pictures on the bills. Little smiley
faces.

Mark   Wow.

Tan   Beat off for him in Times Square, on 41st Street.
Three a.m.

Mark   No cops?

Tan   You'd be surprised. How easy it is to do things and
no one notices. I've had cops walk ten feet away and not
even see. (*Beat.*) So we gonna take a bath together or what?

Mark   Tan.

Tan   I love how you say my name. Gives me a boner.

Mark   Yeah?

Tan   See for yourself. Bathtub! Wheee!

Tan *leaps into the empty bathtub. Only his head and shoulders are visible.*

Mark There's such a light about you, you know. Underneath everything, you have this joy . . .

Tan You could fit your whole bathroom in this tub.

Mark I'm – just not – sure what's happening here, Tan.

Tan Neither am I!

He tosses his shoes out of the tub.

Wheeee!

Mark *laughs.*

Tan They give you free bubble bath.

Tan's *belt comes ripping off.* **Mark** *stares away, at mirror.*

Mark Well, I guess I wonder why. I wonder why you're here and why. Why you don't. Go somewhere for help You're. So young and. You know? It's wrong for me to. Well, just in terms of me I shouldn't – my heart is starting to – hurt and. But. You should get help and if I can.

Tan *laughs. Pants over the edge of the tub. Socks. Underwear.* **Tan** *giggles.* **Mark** *laughs.*

Mark Okay.

Tan *takes off his shirt.*

Mark Well. Do you. Do you have anything to say about what I'm. Saying or?

Tan *stands, back to us, naked. Reaches, dims the light.* **Mark** *looks in the mirror, then closes his eyes.*

Mark Look, I.

He opens his eyes, keeps them vaguely averted.

I got you a Christmas gift, and then I'm going to leave, okay? But I wanted to give you . . .

Mark *puts his sketchpad on the bathtub.*

Tan   Don't go.

He opens the pad.

Wow, it's your drawings. Oh wow. Is that me?

Mark   Yes.

Tan *(flipping through)*   Oh wow.

Mark   Yes.

Tan   Wow.

Mark   You can jerk off if you want to.

Tan   What?

Mark   Okay. And then I'll leave. Okay?

Tan   Okay.

Mark   Lay down. In the tub.

Tan *does. We can't see him.* **Mark** *watches in the mirror.*

Tan   Can you see?

Mark *nods.*

Tan   I like you watching.

Mark   Open your legs a little.

Tan   Makes me feel good.

Mark *watches.*

Scene Six

Apartment. **Stephen**'s *asleep in his bed.* **Petra**'s *at the kitchen table, reading.* **Mark** *enters.*

Petra   Hi.

Mark   Hi. Can I talk to you?

Petra   Sure.

Mark   Is Stephen asleep?

Petra   I think so.

Mark   Come here.

Mark *sits on his couch, wraps himself in a blanket.* **Petra** *comes over, sits on the edge of the couch. He doesn't say anything. He snuggles into her a bit.*

Petra   Are you all right?

Mark   You won't tell Stephen what I tell you, will you?

Petra   Well. No.

Mark   Promise. He'll be mad.

Petra   Are you all right?

Mark   Yeah. No. No I'm not all right. Will you say a prayer with me?

Petra   Sure.

Mark   My heart is just. I have to make all these – I almost – I almost – with Tan tonight – I just – what can I do about my heart? My heart feels like, oh God. I hurt. I *hurt*. What can I do? What can I do?

Petra   I think it's –

Mark   I'm – I want – I want so bad to touch him, I almost – I almost –

Petra   You're shaking.

Mark   It feels – What can I do? – my *heart* –

Petra   I think, Mark. I think the only thing for you to do is stop. Seeing him.

Mark   But he – he has nothing he *needs* me and –

Petra   He doesn't need you.

Mark   I've been so nice to him I can't –

Petra   You don't need him and that's what you need to think about right now.

Mark   No.

Petra   That's – all I can say to you. You can't stop how you feel but you can change what you *do*.

Mark   It felt so good, Petra. It felt so good.

Petra   What? –

Mark   I used to use drugs I don't do that anymore I stopped.

Petra   I know you did and that was hard and I'm sure there was a time you never thought –

He puts his arm around her waist.

Mark   And I think I grew up and how –

Petra   I bet you thought it was impossible –

Mark   – and my heart. It felt so good. I don't feel good. I don't feel good.

Petra   Why don't we, Mark, why don't we say a prayer together.

Mark *moves away from her.*

Petra   Why don't we –

Mark   I need you to leave now.

Pause.

Petra   What?

Mark   You have to go please.

She sits up.

Petra   You want me to leave?

Mark   Yes.

Petra   Well. Okay.

Mark   I'm sorry.

Petra   I'll be in my room if you need anything.

Mark   Thank you.

Petra *goes, off.* **Mark** *stands. He goes to* **Stephen***'s room. He climbs onto the loft bed. He shakes* **Stephen***.*

Mark   Wake up.

Stephen *awakens.*

Stephen   Wha . . . ?

Mark   It's me.

Stephen   Wh— are you okay?

Mark   Hug me.

Stephen   Mark?

Mark *climbs atop* **Stephen** *and hugs him.*

Stephen   Are you – okay? –

Mark   Shhh.

Mark *keeps hugging. Then starts rubbing against* **Stephen***.*

Stephen   Whoa –

Stephen *sits up, pushes* **Mark** *away.*

Mark   What?

Stephen (*still groggy*)   Mark, what?

Mark   Hug me again. Just hug.

Stephen   Mark – are you okay?

Mark   You said I needed anything I could wake you up.

Stephen   I know –

Mark   I was remembering us – how good it felt –

Stephen   Well – yeah –

Mark   – so just hug me, Stephen, hug me.

Stephen   Oh God.

Mark   What?

Stephen   Oh God oh.

Stephen*'s face tightens.*

Mark   What? *What?*

A beat.

Stephen (*flustered*)   I – I came.

Mark   You came?

Stephen   I – Mark –

Mark   You came without? – But you weren't touching yourself –

Stephen   I – I know I . . .

Mark   I want to come.

Stephen   Mark –

Mark   I want to come now.

Stephen   Mark, please – oh God, please let's leave my bed –

Mark   Are you – come on, I want to come, you just came –

Stephen   What's – what's wrong?

Mark   Stephen!

Stephen   Let's just go into the living room.

Mark   One night, once, Stephen.

Mark *buries his head in* **Stephen***'s chest, kisses, fumbles with his jeans.*

Stephen   No, Mark, no, Mark, we can talk, we can *talk* –

He pushes him away.

Mark   I don't want to talk! I'm sick of I don't want to talk!

Stephen   Mark, I want to help you, I want –

Mark *jumps off the bed.*

Mark   I'm leaving, I'm leaving.

Stephen *climbs off the bed.*

Stephen   Mark, you shouldn't go out –

Mark   I didn't touch him, I didn't do anything with him, Stephen –

Stephen   You stay here, I'll go.

Mark   What are you doing? Go where?

Stephen   Just stay here.

Mark   Where are you –

Stephen *goes to the closet, takes clothes, begins putting them on.*

Mark   Where are you going? Stephen. Stephen. Stephen! Don't – where are you going? You can't leave. Stephen – answer me! – don't fucking leave me, Stephen. Don't leave me here –

He blocks **Stephen***'s way.*

Mark   No. No.

Stephen *tries to go,* **Mark** *continues to block.* **Stephen** *pushes* **Mark** *out of the way, exits the bedroom. He puts on his shoes.*

Mark   Where are you going, answer me, answer me, Stephen, Stephen, answer me. Why aren't you ANSWERING me –

Stephen *grabs his backpack. He begins to cry.*

Mark   Stephen – Stephen – I need you right now where
are you – come back here! Come back here! Come back
here!

Stephen *puts on a coat, still crying.*

Mark   Don't – cry, Stephen. Okay. Okay. Look, I'm quiet
now. Look, I'm quiet. I'm okay. You don't know what
happened. We can talk about it. We can talk about what
happened. We can talk just please don't. Come back to bed.
Come back.

Stephen *gets his keys, goes to the door.*

Mark   It's late, Stephen, where – it's Christmas. It's
Christmas. It's Christmas. It's.

Stephen *opens the door.*

Mark   Stephen. Stephen!

Stephen *goes. Door slams.*

Mark   Stephen! –

Mark *begins punching his leg. He stops. His face is blank. His
breathing is heavy.* **Petra** *comes out of her room, listens. Silence.*
Mark *walks to the couch.* **Petra** *quickly sneaks back into her room.*
Mark *takes the cordless phone and goes back to* **Stephen***'s bed. He
dials, presses the phone to his ear, curls into a fetal position.*

Act Three

Scene One

Petra *sits on the couch reading.* **Stephen** *comes storming in.*

Stephen Hi.

Petra When did you get back?

Stephen This morning. So listen. I got fired.

Petra Oh no.

Stephen Yes because. Because someone, because I made up, I wrote the blurb for *Men in Black* without watching it, they *found* out, someone *told* them. Someone, I told some *intern* in the office who I guess *blabbed* it. And literally. They called me into the office and asked me if I'd watched the movie. And. And you know. What am I? – I laugh. I laugh. Because. I say, 'Well,' because I did watch the trailer, I watched the trailer so – so – I mean, come on! So they said, and there's two of them there, my boss and the 'other' boss, the boss I never see, you know, the one who's always out having *lunch* eight hours a day. So what am I going to say, Yes, I did watch it and what, take a POP QUIZ on *Men in Black*?

Petra So what did you say?

Stephen I said I – *fast-forwarded* through it. And they said *That is not good enough*. And I said *Okay*. I'm sitting there. And they said *We're sorry*. And they sent me to *personnel*. And I have credit-card bills, you know, this is not – I'm a – walking down the street. I write blurbs. I am a blurb writer. And you know, I didn't want to watch *Men in Black* that day, you know, and – you would think they'd – find it *funny*. But. So. So. New Year's Eve, here we are. Thank *God* this year is behind me is all I have to say. *Whooosh*. Goodbye. Any word from Mark?

Petra   I haven't seen him.

Stephen   Well, I guess that's it. I guess I'm going to the play alone tonight. Unless you want to . . .

Petra   I can't, I have – I made some plans.

Stephen   Have you seen him at all since I went home?

Petra   He's been here a lot during the day. On the phone.

Stephen   Have you been talking to him?

Petra   No. Listen, you got –

Stephen   Did I do the right thing? That night was just so – maybe I shouldn't have gone home, maybe I should have *stayed* and just forced him to talk . . . his stuff's still here . . .

Petra *hands* **Stephen** *an envelope.*

Stephen   Oh God.

Petra   This is it?

Stephen   This is it. This came today?

Petra   Mm-hmm.

He opens it. He takes out the letter.

Stephen   I got it. I, yeah, I got it. Oh my God. I got it, seven thousand dollars.

Petra   Oh. Yes. Yes.

Stephen   Thank you. Oh my God. Wow! Oh God. That's great. Oh my God.

Petra   Oh, I'm so happy for you.

Stephen   Wow. Wow! Well, that's over. I got it. Done. Oh.

Stephen *grabs the large envelope from the top of the TV.*

Stephen   Look.

Petra   What?

Stephen   He still hasn't opened it.

He puts it back on the TV. He looks at his grant letter again. **Petra** *looks at him and smiles.*

Scene Two

A sleek modern apartment. **Man** *and* **Petra**.

Man   Before we go any further, I want to get this out of the way.

He hands her an envelope. She puts it into her purse.

Now. Now that that's done I want you to know – you can leave anytime you want. Okay?

Petra   Okay.

Man   So. This is it. I know, it could use a woman's touch.

Petra   It's very minimalist.

Man   Well, that's not really by design. My wife kept all the really great stuff. Have a seat.

She sits on a couch.

Do I have plans for us tonight. What's better than a quiet New Year's at home?

Petra   It's such a difficult holiday to do right.

Man   You're telling me! Misery of miseries! I've never had a good New Year's Eve.

Petra   You're kidding! Oh God, me either. There's not one New Year's Eve where I haven't cried.

Man   Well, not tonight. That's the only rule, okay? Now: wine?

Petra   I'd love a glass.

He pours wine.

Man   So first off the bat, tell me how you are.

Petra   I'm okay. Stephen got back today. He got that grant which is very exciting.

Man   Do you realize that whenever I ask how you are, you tell me about someone else?

Pause.

Petra   I'm well, thank you.

Man   I want this to be a good holiday for you. A good New Year's Eve.

Petra *sips wine.*

Man   Tell me what you're writing. Tell me what you've been working on, how about that.

Petra   Well, I've been reading a lot. This excellent book by Mary Gaitskill; and Dorothy Parker, who's very underrated I think. People dismiss her as some sort of alcoholic, you know, little funny poem writer, but. She wrote some devastating fiction. The class issues are . . .

Man   Maybe you can lend me her book.

Petra   Yes. Listen. I. I don't want to take your money. Not tonight.

Man   Anyway. Listen. I want to read you a poem.

Petra   I'm serious –

Man   Not now. Here.

Petra *sips wine.*

Man   Okay. This isn't easy. Okay.

'The darkness of your eyes
pierces into my heart.
I cannot fathom the size
of the waters you part.
You contain such light

that I cannot even see.
But I shall take flight
in your utter beauty.'

There. I said it. Okay. Be honest. Tell me. I know,
rhyming's kind of passé, right?

Petra   I'm – very glad you wrote that. I hope. I hope it
gave you some joy.

Man   It's about you.

Petra   That . . . makes me feel good.

The **Man** *smiles.*

Scene Three

The apartment. **Stephen***'s sitting, reading.* **Mark** *enters.*

Mark   Hi.

Stephen   Hi. Are you . . . the play starts in half an hour,
are you? . . .

Mark   Oh no. I have this – party to go to. I'm – sorry, I
forgot all about it.

Stephen   Well – we haven't spoken since – so . . . I um – I
should get going but I thought –

Mark   I just came to pick something up.

He crosses to the large envelope atop the TV, takes it.

. . . Are you going to the play alone?

Stephen   Yeah.

Mark   Cool. You went home to see your folks Pet said,
how um. How was that?

Stephen   It was good. Actually. As good as . . . you know.

Mark   Yeah. Well.

Stephen   Right.

Mark   Happy New Year's.

Stephen   You too.

Mark *goes. Door slams.* **Stephen** *crosses to his jacket. He puts it on. He goes to the door. He waits some moments. And goes.*

Scene Four

The Royalton bathroom. They've set a TV and VCR up on the sink counter. **Mark** *and* **Tan** *are watching, passing a cigarette between them. They sit in the giant tub. We can see they are bare-chested. Sounds from TV.*

Tan   Man. Yeah. Yeah.

Mark   Hah. Yeah, I shot that, that was fun.

Tan   What was he like, in real life?

Mark   He was whatever.

Mark *uses an eye-dropper to drop a few darkish drops of liquid into his nose. He hands the eye-dropper to* **Tan**, *who gives him the cigarette.*

Tan   This is totally cool, man.

Mark   Yeah. I feel good. I feel good. Did I tell you about the bathroom in the place I looked at? Practically identical to this one . . . 'cept not mirrors like these but . . .

Tan (*finishing with the drops*)   You know what I was thinking.

Mark   What?

Tan   I was thinking it'd be cool to come, you know, as the clock hits twelve or whatever.

Mark   Yeah?

Tan   Yeah. You don't think that's cheesy, do you?

Mark   No. I think it's kind of hot.

Tan   Yeah.

He takes **Mark***'s hand with the cigarette, brings it to his mouth, inhales. Lets go.*

Tan   Whoa! Butch camera angle! Fuck! That dude, what's his name? He's cool.

Scene Five

Man*'s apartment.* **Petra***'s a little tipsy.*

Petra   You know what people want? I'll tell you, you, me, Quentin Tarantino, Bill Clinton, whether they know it or not, I'll tell you exactly what people want: love. As stupid as that sounds.

Man   Hah, you're getting drunk, I've never seen you like this.

Petra   No, we're all the same, in this, in just this one way, look, look: they have on videotape of, they have children, they did this in Britain, this study, okay, and little kids would get beaten up by their mothers, little, two and three years old, slapped, punched, disgusting – but when the nurse came into the room – they actually did this, secret videotape – when the nurse came in to stop the beating and take the baby from the abusive mother, the baby cried, the baby cried and tried to hang on to its mother. So. So whatever you want to call it, that's – the baby wants – love – so the love is inappropriate, so what, it's what the baby knows.

Man (*laughing*)   And some babies grow up to make movies and run countries.

Petra *laughs, refills her wine glass.*

Man   You sure about that?

Petra I'm not drunk. Okay. You asked me once, you said
are you in pain? And I lied. I said no. And I'm in pain
because I am not loved. You see. And artists – there's so
little love to go around – the promise of love is so fleeting
and inconsistent so to get noticed – people do – what they *do*
is – just like you cheated on your wife, you see it in art too,
the terror of not being loved, safe art, meaningless art,
pandering art, commercial art, titillating art, outrageous art,
can we sell it, can I sell myself, will I be rewarded with
money, with prestige, with recognition – all those things
which are, which are *perversions* of love – and let me tell you.
If there were more love to go around. And more
consciousness and less fear. People might make beautiful
things. Beautiful things. What are all these horrible
disgusting movies with violence and anger and, you know, I
mean, they're cries for help! You look at a Quentin
Tarantino movie, you know, This man has never been
loved. He has had no experience of love in his life. Art, the
art can never be better than the person who made it.

Man Well, you have to love yourself, don't you? Isn't that
the hardest part?

Petra You know what? That's New Age bullshit. You
can't love yourself. You go and try. One is a fiction. Reality
exists when the other person walks into the room. Life is
other people.

Man So is hell, or so someone said.

Petra Well then, so is heaven.

Man Do you think you'll be loved?

Petra I'd better.

Man Do you think you will?

Petra Hey, if I didn't, I'd put my head in the oven.

Man Me too. Hah. That calls for one more glass, I think.
We're not even close to the ball dropping, you know.

Man *pours himself a drink.* **Petra** *gets up, goes to a rack of CDs.*

Petra   Okay, tell me you have more than Bob Dylan.

Man   Van Morrison.

Petra   Shut up, what do you have to dance to?

Man   Oh God. Dance?

Petra   Yeah, you're gonna dance with me.

Man   Dance.

Petra   Here we go.

Petra *puts on a slow, sexy Janet Jackson song. She starts to dance.*

Man   Wow, look at you.

Petra   Come on, get up here.

He does.

Man   I can't believe I'm doing this.

He starts to dance. **Petra** *laughs.*

Petra   See! You're great!

Man   Don't mock me!

Petra   You're great!

She moves closer to **Man**, *dances.*

Come on, just let go.

Man   That's very hard for insecure people.

Petra   You're good! God, I love dancing.

Man   You do, eh.

Petra   The only orgasms I've had, the last two years –
while I've been dancing.

Man   You're joking.

Petra   Only when I've been dancing. And I've been in plenty of beds in that time.

Man   Really, when you're stripping?

Petra   Mm-hmm. See, now you're dancing!

Man   Don't condescend.

Petra   I'm not. Here, you have to look at the person when you're dancing.

Petra *grabs him and slow-dances.*

Man   Whoa.

Petra   When's the last time you danced?

Man   My wedding night, I think.

Petra   So you don't have herpes, do you?

Man *stops a little, then starts up again.*

Man   Well, why do you ask?

Petra   Answer the question, come on.

Man   No. No, I don't. Have it.

Petra *laughs. They dance.*

Man   Nothing gets by your artist's eye, does it?

Petra   I want to go to your bed.

Man   You want to go to my bed?

Petra   Yes.

Man   No you don't.

Petra   Yes I do.

Man   Well, I don't want to.

Petra *smiles, dances a few steps longer, then stops.* **Man** *stops.*

Man   I mean – you're gorgeous but. But. That's not right. You shouldn't – maybe you had a little too much to drink –

Petra   You know, I'm not a child, three, four glasses of wine, I am *conscious*. It's not like I popped a Rohypnol too.

Man   I'm sorry.

Petra   You're sorry? You're – fuck you.

Man   Whoa, what?

Petra   Fuck you you're sorry you – you invite me to your apartment and – New Year's Eve – and you tell me I'm beautiful and you write a –

Man   Wait, I never said – I never, I was always up front –

Petra   No, you manipulative you, no you made me – you made me – no –

Man   – about what I wanted, I was always honest with you. I was always. Here. Sit. Sit. You're drunk.

Petra *sits back down.*

Man   I'm sorry. Oh God.

Petra *takes a deep breath.*

Man   Listen. Listen I just wanted to talk to you. I just – I never wanted this to –

Petra *stands.*

Petra   You know what, I'm just gonna go home.

Man   Are you sure?

Beat.

Petra   Yeah. Yeah I'm sure.

Man   I'll talk to you . . .

Petra   Well, look at us. Look at this, you know.

Pause. **Man** *goes to the stereo, shuts off the music.*

Man   You – you should be having a blast. I wanted you to have a good New Year's Eve. I'm sorry.

Petra   No, this is. This is a good New Year's Eve.
Actually. If you can believe it.

Petra *laughs.*

Man   Let me call you a car.

She reaches into her pocketbook and takes out the envelope.

Petra   Look, I can't, and I don't want to, take this.

Man   No. No. You. I think you're valuable. I value you
and you, you should go out there and. Make something
beautiful.

She looks at him. She puts the envelope back in her pocketbook.

Petra   You're gonna make me cry.

Man   No! Don't cry! Listen, let me call you a car.

He goes to the phone, across the room.

Hi, I need a car at 178 East 72nd Street. Yes. To the East
Village. Yes.

Petra *begins to cry, silently.*

Man   To um – what's the street address? Petra?

Petra   – 199 East 4th.

Man   To 199 East 4th. Yeah, 178 East 72nd. Thanks!

He hangs up.

They'll be right there.

She turns. She walks to him and gives him a hug.

Oh – oh – you're crying.

Petra   I'm okay.

Man   You're sure?

Petra   Yeah.

She lets go. Laughs, wipes away tears.

God, my accent comes out so bad when I cry.

A beat.

Man   I am gonna watch me some Dick Clark tonight.

They share a brief laugh.

The car'll be right down.

Petra *nods.*

Petra   Goodbye.

Man   I'll uh – I'll keep an eye out for you. In the papers, I mean. I don't imagine I'll be seeing you – at the club. So. I'll. Good luck with everything.

Petra   Thank you. You too.

Petra *goes.*

Scene Six

The Royalton bathroom. Post-coital, on the tile floor.

Mark   Oh God.

Tan   You fuck like someone who hasn't fucked in a really long time.

Mark   Yeah, well. Before this . . . it was a really long time.

Tan   You're good.

Mark   You too.

He kisses **Tan** *on the head.*

Mark   I'm cold. I'm gonna put on some clothes.

Tan, *naked, turns on the TV.* **Mark** *starts to dress.*

Tan   Hey, dude, you're putting on my pants.

Mark   Oh yeah. Whoops. Oh well. See how I look.

He puts on the tight jeans. Really tight.

I'm Tan. Hello.

*He takes **Tan**'s wallet out of his pants, opens it.*

Let's see here.

Tan   Whoa, whoa –

Mark *stops. Takes out a small card.*

Tan   – Well. Guess um.

Mark   You go to NYU?

Tan   Well, yeah. Yeah.

Tan *grabs a shirt –* **Mark**'s *– and throws it on.*

Mark   Huh.

Tan   Yeah, so.

He grabs pants, puts them on.

Mark   Whatever.

Mark *grabs* **Tan**'s *shirt, puts it on.*

Tan   What, you're not – mad?

Mark   No.

Tan   You're not?

Mark   I figured as much, I mean. It doesn't matter.

Tan (*face erupting into a smile*)   Really?

Mark   Yeah.

Tan   Hey, you know I major, I major in acting.

Mark   Yeah?

Tan   Yeah, so, if you make any more movies . . .

Mark *smiles, nods, hands* **Tan** *his wallet. Looking at TV:*

Tan   Shit, it's ten minutes.

Mark   What?

Tan   Till the ball drops.

Mark   Oh.

Tan   We forgot. We finished too early.

Mark (*chuckles*)   Oops.

Tan   Wanna see if we can come? At midnight, we can try anyway? We can just, like, jerk off.

Mark   Um. Okay. What the hell.

Tan   'Cuz I think that'd be cool. To come at midnight.

Mark   Fun.

Tan   We could even do it by the window. People could see us. No one could tell who we were, and it'd be a kick, right?

Mark   Do it by the window?

Tan   And then people could see us.

Scene Seven

The apartment. **Stephen**'s *on the couch.* **Petra** *enters. We hear party noise from the street and from other apartments within the building.*

Petra   Hey.

Stephen   Why are you home? It's not midnight?

Petra   I'll be right back.

She goes into her room.

(*Off.*) I was thinking about what you said. About starting the New Year on a symbolic note. So I thought I'd come home and. Read or something.

Stephen   Oh. Well, that's nice. I'm glad you're here.

Petra (*off*)   What?

Stephen   I'm glad you're here!

Some moments pass. **Petra** *comes into the living room, wrapped in a kimono. She sits on the couch.*

Stephen   Was your night okay?

Petra   Yeah.

Stephen   Yeah. Mine too. I'm sad.

Petra   Me too.

Stephen   But it'll be okay.

Petra   Yeah. It'll be okay.

Pause.

Will you be mad at me if I leave, Stephen?

Stephen   Leave where?

Petra   If I leave here.

Stephen   You're going to leave?

Petra   I'm going to leave this city.

Stephen   You are?

Petra *nods.*

Stephen   Where are you going to go?

Petra   I don't know yet.

Stephen   When?

Petra   Soon.

Pause.

Stephen   Wow.

Petra   Yeah.

Stephen   You never said anything. When did you decide this?

Petra   I've been thinking about it for a long time.

Pause.

Stephen   I'll miss you.

Petra   I'll miss you. How was the play?

Stephen *shrugs. Pause. Noise from outside.*

Stephen   What time is it?

Petra   Oh God, there's one minute.

Stephen   Eleven fifty-nine.

Petra   Should we turn on the TV and watch all the people in Times Square and watch the ball drop?

Stephen   No.

Pause.

Petra   I'm gonna go read.

Pause. **Petra** *gets up, goes off to her room.* **Stephen** *stays seated. Outside, we hear continued sounds of people, shouting, honking, stomping around, screaming.* **Stephen** *does not move. We hear people counting down from ten.* **Stephen** *closes his eyes. The sounds increase.*

The Coming World

Sure, what do you care for money? You'd give your last penny to the first beggar you met, if he had a shotgun pointed at your heart.

Eugene O'Neill, *A Moon for the Misbegotten*

. . . This music's almost unrecognizable, so utterly of the coming world it is.

Mark Doty, 'Tunnel Music'

The Coming World was first performed at Soho Theatre,
London, on 3 April 2001. The cast was as follows:

Ed   Andrew Scott
Dora   Doraly Rosen
Ty   Andrew Scott

Director Mark Brickman
Designer Michael Pavelka
Lighting Designer Jason Taylor
Movement Liz Rankin

Characters

Ed, *mid-twenties*
Dora, *late twenties*
Ty, *mid-twenties*

Ed and **Ty** are played by the same actor.

No interval.

Setting
Summer, on a beach off the coast of New England.

A Note on the Design

I am not a designer but it is, I think, worth noting that as I
wrote this play, I imagined it taking place on a bare stage
(no sand!), with no costume change or use of makeup effects,
etc. While the play may benefit from a careful nod towards
more traditional design elements, it's important that they
not overwhelm the text which, I think, can tell us more than
showing can.

  In the London production there were no sound effects or
music; no makeup effects; basic lighting, bright (though the
play takes place largely at night); and a mostly bare stage
made of gray wooden planks. Scenes in the ocean were
created by taking out all lights; the actors held thin
flashlights which washed light over their bodies. What I
would stress most is that the play mustn't get lost in darkness

and night. The text tells the audience it's evening; the lights should let us see clearly those evenings play out.

A Note on the Text:

A slash (/) indicates when the following speech begins. In the second scene, I use punctuation to convey a sense of the unspoken. The meaning should be clear to both the actors and the audience, while maintaining the idiosyncratic and intimate system of communication the lovers use in their distress. Sometimes it's used to portray a gap in communication, a pregnant nonspoken moment different from a flat pause. Other times, a manner of speech is conveyed. For instance, if the dialogue in the text reads

Dora (You said)   What?
the actress would speak, and the audience would hear

Dora   What?
The parentheses are meant to clarify the meaning of what is actually spoken (rather than implied), to avoid a situation where an actor would say

Dora   What?
and the audience would understand it to mean
Dora   What (do you mean)?

Scene One

The beach. **Dora** *and* **Ed** *are laughing.*

Ed   Come on, dare me.

Dora   'Dare' you!

Ed   Fifty more! (*Flicking a little handful of sand at her.*) Come /
on!

Dora (*laughing*)   Ah! Don't throw sand at me! – Go ahead,
torture yourself.

Ed   Here we go. One . . .

Ed *does push-ups.* **Dora** *brushes sand out of her hair.*

Dora   Hey, the DVDs are coming in a couple weeks, they
called today.

Ed   No shit!

Dora   They're starting slow, building them in slow. They
did a survey, I guess, and not that many people here have
DVD players yet.

Ed   Yeah, 'cuz there's no fucking place to buy DVDs!
What am I at, forty?

Dora   Yeah, *right*. That's gonna be a pain, though,
building them in, we're gonna have to totally rearrange the
store to make room for new shelves.

Ed *stops and catches his breath.*

Ed   What are we doing tonight?

Dora   I dunno. Why don't we just stay on the beach, it's
nice.

Ed   You're not working tomorrow, right?

Dora   At night I am. I'm closing.

Ed   Get some drinks?

Dora   We could watch a movie . . .

Ed   Go out, have a couple gin and tonics . . .

Dora   When is it ever 'a couple'. All night.

Ed   I'm not saying all night. Plus – Martin's gonna be out tonight.

Dora   Martin?

Ed *starts doing push-ups again.*

Ed   You remember Martin.

Dora   Yeah, no shit. Why, what about him?

Ed   They're hiring. He said – at the – they need money / runners.

Dora   You're not gonna fucking work at the casino.

Ed   Maybe – not, like, right away. But – enough time's passed, right?

Dora   Every day going there?

Ed   The pay is so good. They're hiring. Where / else –

Dora   So, if you gamble it, so, who cares how much the pay is, you know?

Ed   Gambling wasn't – it was the coke that was the thing. The gambling wasn't – I don't even like gambling. Plus I feel *so* much better now –

Dora   That's what I'm saying, you're feeling so much better, so why put yourself back there?

Pause.

Ed   It's just drinks, I mean – I don't even know – it's not like I got the job.

Dora   No, I don't wanna go out drinking tonight.

Pause.

Ed   All right. The thing is . . .

Dora   You told Martin already.

Pause.

So cancel.

Ed   Dora –

Dora   No, I worked all day, I don't / wanna –

Ed   I can't just / blow him off.

Dora   So go without me.

Ed   No . . .

Pause.

Dora   Why not?

Ed   'Cuz I wanna be with you tonight.

Pause.

Dora   All right . . .

Ed   Uh-oh. Dora's got an idea.

Dora   I'll go out for drinks if you call Ty and invite him out.

Pause.

Ed   Why?

Dora   I wanna meet him! Eight months, your twin brother and I have no idea what he's / like.

Ed   He's not gonna come out.

Dora   Why not?

Ed   He doesn't go out.

Dora   Tell him I want to meet him. – I wanna meet the guy!

Pause. **Ed** *looks at the ocean. Then turns to* **Dora** *and smiles. Grabs* **Dora**'s *foot and kisses it, bites it a little. She moans quietly. He licks her foot. She begins to laugh.*

Ed   What's so funny?

He tickles her foot, she shrieks, laughs.

Dora   No!

Ed   No? No?

He embraces her.

Dora   Stop! You're all smelly!

Ed   I'm smelly?

Dora   Yes!

Ed   Then I guess I'm gonna make *you* all smelly!

Dora   No!

He tickles her, she shrieks with laughter. Then he stops. Then he tickles her again, she shrieks with laughter. Then he stops. He starts to tickle her again, she laughs less, as though exhausted. He stares at her a beat, then looks out at the ocean. She follows his gaze to the ocean.

Ed   Beautiful.

Dora   It is . . .

Ed *turns to her.*

Ed   No. You. You have the most beautiful face.

Pause. **Dora** *smiles, then turns away.*

Ed   Okay.

He playfully smacks her thigh.

Call my weirdo brother for you.

Scene Two

The beach. **Dora** *approaches* **Ed**. *She startles him; he jerks.*

Dora   Ahh!

Ed   Shit!

Dora   Ed!

Ed   Sorry.

Dora   Jesus.

Ed   Sorry.

Ed *looks at* **Dora**, *smiles.*

Dora   (   ).

Pause.

Ed   (   )?

Dora   I don't wanna be here.

Ed   I know –

Dora   I can't get in your shit now –

Ed   Nothing for you to get into . . . Sit.

Dora   I'm just – if you want something (just tell me now) . . .

Ed   All I want – serious – all I want is to just . . . (   ) . . .

She doesn't sit.

Miss you. – Okay that I say that?

Dora   (You) Just did.

Ed   Yeah.

Dora   You look bad.

Ed   I look *bad?*

Dora   Yeah.

Ed   It's dark!

Dora   What?

Ed   I look bad (in the dark)?

Dora (*sitting*)   Circles under your eyes, unshaven . . .

Ed   Really?

Dora   Are you . . . (on drugs)?

Ed   No.

Dora   No?

Ed   You look good.

Dora   I worked all day, I look tired.

Ed   How was work?

Dora   (You wanna talk about) Work?

Ed   What movies came in today?

Dora   They come in Tuesdays.

Ed   You put them up Tuesdays, but you get them before.

Dora   (   ).

Pause.

Ed   (I'll) Rub your feet.

Dora   (No).

Ed   Shoulders. You look tense.

Dora   I don't (want a massage).

Ed   Stressed out, standing all day, the kids, annoying, come on.

Dora   Not everyone hates their job.

Ed   Thanks.

Dora   'The kids, annoying' – (actually) I like my job.

Ed   Good for you. (   )?

Dora   – I'm just saying, you're making it like I hate my job.

Ed   I just said do you want a massage that place stresses you out.

Pause.

Dora   You have to stop calling me.

Pause.

Ed   Who's talking about this.

Dora   We broke up.

Ed   Okay.

Dora   Okay?

Ed   I just wanted to talk. Am I doing anything?

Dora   'Can I rub your feet.'

Ed   ?

Dora   You don't do the same things after you break up. You don't (give massages) –

Ed   – I don't even feel bad.

Dora   (   )?

Ed   Not about you. Something else. I mean I do (feel bad) about you. But I don't know if I (feel bad) about this other thing. Maybe after I say it I'll feel bad. – No one knows (what I did).

Dora   What are you talking / about?

Ed   Why do you think Ty won't talk to me?

Dora   (   ).

Ed   He won't call me back. Since we hung out. Which. That was a fun night. He had fun, right?

Dora   (Like) You remember (that night).

Ed   It was only a month ago.

Dora   No. Because you blacked out. (I was) Dragging you home.

Ed   (You didn't) Drag me home.

Dora   Yeah (right)!

Ed   He's probably just heavy into work. Computer shit. Big money. I thought it was maybe the money (he lent me) but that doesn't make sense. Why he would be mad about that.

Dora   (   )?

Ed   He lent me money. I think he sent it, I think he sent it the next day, day after we hung out. We were broke up when I got the check so I didn't tell you but. In the mail. Five thousand dollars. (I was like) Shit! Five thousand dollars! Just in my mail! No note, no anything, and so – I called him, to like – I don't know, to thank him or to say (Why did you send me five thousand dollars) . . . (I keep) Calling, but he won't call me back. – Why did I get so drunk that night?

Dora   He just – (sent you) five thousand dollars.

Pause.

(I hope) You don't need more.

Ed (*laughs*)   Why do you say that?

Dora   Because – you don't look so good, you don't look a guy who has five thousand dollars, so – (do you need more?) . . .

Ed *reaches into his pocket, takes out ten singles.*

Dora   What (are you doing)?

Ed   Ten dollars.

Dora   (I know) But (why)?

Ed   (This is) All I have left.

Pause.

Dora   (   )?

Ed   It went.

Dora   I don't (understand).

Ed   Paid bills, paid – not like five's a fortune, I mean, what I owe. I was just trying to set things up, climb outta this hole –

Dora   The thousand (I gave you, is that gone too)?

Ed   I paid off the credit card (with that).

Dora   Where did it (go)?

Ed   . . .

Dora   I'm not (giving you anything) – Nothing.

Ed   I had a job.

Dora   ?

Ed   (I got paid a) Thousand a week.

Dora   . . .

Ed   You want me to jump to the end of the story or start at the start of it?

Dora   I don't (care).

Ed   It's just, I don't know which way (makes more sense) – starting and going forward or going to the end and then back. Makes sense – (not the story, but) telling you.

Dora   I'm not going to get all (wrapped up in it) . . .

Ed   But do you want to hear just the outcome or how I got there? . . .

Dora   It's not gonna make me do something (I'm not gonna do).

Ed   (Do you know) I'm the only person Ty ever showed his tattoos to? I ever tell you that?

Dora   This (relates how)? . . .

Ed   I'm just – trying to talk like – like there's none of this shit in between us.

Dora   (So you lost) Five thousand dollars.

Ed   You think I should get a tattoo?

Dora   – They're gross.

Ed   Why?

Dora   It's like self-mutilation, they're ugly.

Ed   Ty showed me his. I'm the only one.

Dora   Ed. Come on.

Ed *looks at her. Pause.*

Ed   Okay. All right. (I'll tell you) What happened.

Pause.

Dora   I don't need all kinds of details.

Ed   All right.

Pause. She turns.

I just – there's this one question to get – out of the way – so I can tell you what happened because, just – I . . .

Pause.

Dora   ?

Ed   . . .

Dora   . . . ?

Ed   No, I know (why you broke up with me). I had no
money. What you (said), I have no (money), I'm in debt, I
have no job, you can't be with someone (with) no money
(and) no job . . . But – if there's (another reason) – you can
tell me, I just (wanna know) –

Dora   No, there's no other reason, Ed.

Ed   All right, okay, that's all I wanted (to know) . . .

She looks out at the ocean.

Okay. Okay. So. There's this (guy). I'm in the (casino) – at
the least, I promise you, this is a good story.

Dora (*turning back to him*)   Then (start telling it).

Ed   No, because you look like (you don't care) –

Dora   I'm (listening, just tell me).

Ed   I'm just (saying) – . . . Okay. – I haven't even told this
(to anyone). Okay.

I'm in the casino chilling, and this guy says there's this guy
he knows. And the guy, the guy I'm talking to –

Dora   ?

Ed   (Okay,) Martin.

Dora   Martin (, great).

Ed   Don't get all stupid.

Dora   Fucking Martin.

Ed   Martin and John.

Dora   (I don't know) John (, who is he)?

Ed   They just know each other. John's at the casino all the
time, Martin knows him from there. Okay. So Martin tells
me John, John needs somebody for something – under-the –
quick-buck thing. Puts me in (touch) – Martin – with John –
in touch so – okay? Okay. So: what do I have to lose? I
figure (what the hell, who knows) – so – okay. I call John.

Hello, hello, come over, so. I go over. House, *his* house, oh
my God. It's (fucking amazing) – totally new, mile away
(from the casino) – inside – big TV, flat-screen, DVD. Guys
watching *The Matrix* – the scene (where Neo fights the guy in
the subway) – John sits me down, this *other* guy, guy gets
me a drink, and I'm – (sitting) on this like electronic plush
chair – massage, adjust the –

Dora   (What are all) These details . . .

Ed   (Sorry, I'm getting all excited.) Okay. So. Okay. So
John's like, a big guy, maybe thirty, well groomed, but, like,
hairy back kind of guy. (He's) Mob (and he's like –)

Dora   ?

Ed   But (not scary).

Dora   Mob.

Ed   (All right, but) He says, 'It's a very simple thing, Ed.'
Simple. I'm like – (it's) like a movie, (I'm) sitting there, like –
'I supply' – this is him – 'I' –

Dora   You don't have to get all dramatic.

Ed   (You don't think it's funny?) – Okay.

'I supply a local man with Ecstasy. He distributes it to his
people at six schools. I don't like to be involved with drugs
but it's a lot of money and this is as far as I go with it. It's
safe, it's easy, it's very lucrative. What your job is is this:' –
and I'm sitting there, with my drink, thinking like (is this
really happening?) – 'Your job is this:' – not would be, (but)
is – 'once a week, you'll deliver the Ecstasy to this man.
You'll be paid a thousand for each delivery. All you do is
come here, pick up a backpack with ten thousand dollars of
pills, drive half an hour, hand it over, take the cash, bring it
back, I'll cut you a thousand, and you'll go home.'

Pause.

I mean, problem solved! Before Christmas! Four thousand a
month!

Dora   So you just (say yes) . . .

Ed   (I know but) I think – what if he knows some other
guy, more eager guy, I don't want to (lose the chance) –
Martin (must know other guys but) – he thought of me first.
John's like, 'Martin speaks very highly of you.'

Dora   Martin speaks highly of you. Which, he knows you
from (what). 'He's a good drinker. He sniffs coke and loses
money really well.'

Ed   (Fuck you).

Dora   ( ).

Ed   ( ).

Dora   Five minutes (you know this guy) and you say yes.

Ed   I thought – he needs his money – drugs need to get
where they're going – (it's) simple how I fit in. John said he
doesn't like his guys to do it because if you get caught it's
mandatory minimum sentence, so he contracts it out to keep
it out of his thing. He said no one ever got caught but it's
better for him that he's not directly connected to it.

Dora   Fine, so. What. (Happened).

Ed *pauses, staring at* **Dora**.

Dora   ( )?

Ed   Okay. So. Next day. I get the backpack. They give me
a phone number. (Of) The guy I'm handing over to. I'm
supposed to go to the payphone in the parking lot of the
bank near the Burger King. I call and let it ring. I can only
use that payphone because what the guy is going to do is, is
look at his caller ID, and when he sees that payphone
number, he's gonna come meet me at the bank. That way
there's no talking on any phones. So. I get the backpack. I
get in my car and go. Get to the Burger King, the bank, pull
in, pull around back –

Dora   (Wait,) What time is it?

Ed   What?

Dora   Is it dark?

Short pause.

This is the phone, the one behind the bank, out of sight of the road?

Ed   There's – the Burger King –

Dora   There's the fence between the bank and the Burger King. And it's dark. (Do you see?)

Ed   What are you (saying)?

Dora   (You're sitting where) No one can see you.

Ed   Why would you want anyone to see?

Dora   (It's a) Backpack – you could hand it over in the Burger/King!

Ed   You wanna tell the story? You know what happens?

Dora   (   ).

Pause.

Ed   (So I) Pick up the phone. Dial. Ringing. Then (I hear) a tap on the glass. (Out of) Nowhere. (I) Look. (It's a) Gun. Passenger side, guy with a gun, tapping on the glass. (I) Turn around, (my) window's rolled down, (I) still have the phone to my ear, sitting in the car, so my window is down, (I) turn. Another guy. (Guy) *Rips* the phone from my hand, hangs it up, slams it . . .
(I) Give him the (backpack) . . .
They just (go) . . .

Pause. **Dora** *looks away.*

So.

Dora   Do you know what happened?

Ed (*grabbing stomach*)   Fuck, my stomach. Can you hear that?

Dora   What?

Ed   I guess only I can hear it, 'cuz of the vibrations in my body.

Dora   What are you talking about?

Ed   My stomach is making weird noises, it hurts.

Dora   – Ed, they didn't see the caller ID, so how did they know what time you were gonna be there?

Ed   I guess – I figure John probably told them around when to expect me. So they were probably just hanging out, waiting. Waiting for a car to pull in there, pick up the phone. Boom.

Dora   But . . . you don't see?

Ed   (   )?

Dora   Okay. So – Martin and John know each other a little, they bullshit, whatever. One night John says to Martin, 'Hey, Martin, I need a favor.' Martin's flattered, (he's a) bartender, (and a) mob guy needs his help. (He) Says, 'Want you to find me some kid, some fuck-up who needs some money. I'll jerk him around, scare him a little, but I won't hurt him, you have my word. You know anybody?' (You.) Now, John's got this all planned out already with the guy – the distributor guy, the dealer. John fills him in, the dealer gives him nine thousand bucks. The *dealer* gets to save a thousand, and now John has an errand boy who thinks he owes him ten thousand bucks. Who'll do whatever he wants.

Ed   What . . . ?

Dora   (They) Pumped you up, gave you a bullshit story – the whole thing was planned out. Robbing *you* works out for both of them, they *both* save all this money, meanwhile, *you* get a gun in your face, and now *you* think you owe a mobster ten thousand bucks. Which, if he says you do, you do. So now he'll make you work it off, doing all his dirty work or whatever.

Ed   I don't . . . you think he set me up? But – no. No way. John – no, there's gotta be holes in there.

Dora   There's no holes.

Ed   (   ).

Short pause.

Oh – oh fuck –

Dora   They're not stupid, these guys, they know what they're doing. This dealer is gonna rob a mobster? No one robs mobsters. They have a whole system, this whole thing together, and this guy's just gonna up and rob him? It's where he gets the Ecstasy from – like you said, they both need each other.

Ed   Oh God.

Pause.

Dora   (Tell me the truth,) Are you doing coke?

Ed   Not – really, I don't know, a couple of times –

Dora   Five thousand dollars partying.

Ed   I haven't (been partying that much), I've been paying (off my debts) – *you* doing coke?

Dora   (We're) Talking about me now?

Ed   Don't be so angry.

Dora   Fine, (let's) talk about me, what do *you* want *me* to do?

Pause.

Ed   (   ).

Dora   So I can just leave now.

Ed   All right. This is what I came up with. I thought – I
can move home, (that) kills my rent, (that) kills my bills. I
gotta pay John, God knows what he's gonna make me do to
pay it off. So, get the ten thousand out of the way, hold off
my other debts –

Dora   So, what, this ten thousand is just gonna wash up
on shore?

Ed   Well – I gotta find a job. Obviously.

Dora   How do I fit into this?

Ed   Well . . . I know I can't – stay with you.

Dora   You already figured that out, you're gonna stay
with your folks.

Ed   Right.

Pause.

I know . . . you don't have any money I could . . . (   ) . . .

Dora   (   ).

Ed   I know.

Dora   So all that's left that I can do for you is fuck you,
basically.

Ed   (Seriously)?

Dora   !

Ed   Kidding, Dora! I'm not (that dumb). But what's going
on with you, you seeing anybody?

Dora   (   ).

Ed   I hope he's good to you, that's all I hope.

Dora   (I) Got it.

Ed   What?

Dora   Ask Ty for more money.

Ed   No.

Dora   Why not?

Ed   That's not right.

Dora   Why not?

Ed   No!

Dora   He gave you five thousand.

Ed   I didn't ask for it. He just gave it to me.

Dora   So?

Ed   What I don't understand is. Because you said you loved me. So when? How do you just stop? Two people / who –

Dora   (   ).

Ed   If you loved me one month / ago –

Dora   Ed –

Ed   Do you love me?

Pause.

Did you?

Dora   (   ).

Ed   ?

Dora   Yes (, but) –

Ed   So when did you stop?

Dora   (   ).

Pause.

Ed   I'm sorry.

Dora   I'm gonna / leave, Ed.

Ed   Okay, wait. Wait. I got this idea. It's a way you can help me. It's a really good idea.

Dora *looks at* **Ed**. **Ed** *looks at* **Dora**.

Ed   I wanna. Okay. Ready?

Dora   (   ).

Ed   I wanna rob the Blockbuster.

Dora   – What?

Ed   How much is it before you put the final night's total in the safe?

Dora   Ed.

Ed   Corporation, won't feel a thing. A couple thousand, right? At closing, so easy, just you in the store –

Dora   No, Ed!

Ed   I know there's all those cameras and stuff, but I put on a mask or whatever, we make it look like an actual robbery, like, with a gun and stuff, simple!

Dora   A *gun?*

Ed   I have one. I got one.

Dora   You have a *gun?*

Ed   What if I get into trouble with John? (What if I have to do) Some ghetto shit?

Pause.

Dora   I'm going, Ed.

Ed   You're gonna go. You're just gonna go.

Dora (*rising*)   Yeah.

Ed   All right. Whatever. (*Starts removing clothes.*) Thanks for the help!

Dora   What are you doing?

Ed   (I'm gonna) Take a swim. You wanna?

Dora   Fuck you.

Dora *starts to exit.* **Ed** *stands naked, laughs.*

Ed   You know you want me. That's why you're leaving!

Dora *keeps going till she is off.*

Ed (*calling*)   You know that's why you're leaving! Come on, come swimming with me.

Pause. **Dora** *is off.*

Ed (*yelling*)   WHY DON'T YOU COME BACK HERE AND COME SWIMMING WITH ME.
WHY DON'T YOU COME BACK AND SUCK MY DICK LIKE YOU USED TO!

Long pause. He's still watching.

(*Screaming*)   WHY DON'T YOU COME BACK AND TELL ME YOU LOVE ME.

Hold.

Scene Three

Ty *approaches* **Dora** *on the beach, tentatively.*

Ty   Dora?

She turns, startled.

Dora   Oh – I didn't . . .

She stands with some difficulty.

Hey, Ty.

Ty   Hi. – Are you okay?

Dora   I'm okay.

Ty   Jesus.

Dora   It's not that bad. They got me on Vicodin, so . . .

Ty   What happened?

Dora You don't know? You didn't hear?

Ty   No.

Dora The Blockbuster got robbed.

Pause.

Ty   Oh.

Dora Didn't get any money actually. But I got roughed up . . .

Ty   Oh my God.

Dora I thought everybody heard.

Ty   No, I . . .

Dora Don't talk to anybody?

Ty (*smiles*)   Right.

Dora *sits, with some difficulty.*

Dora I figured your parents would have told you. Just some random thing – it happens – just happened to happen to me, so.

Ty   Does it hurt?

Dora Just normal pain.

Ty   What's normal pain?

Dora Just – you know. Pain you can live with.

Short pause.

I just – wanted to talk to someone.

Ty   Sure.

Dora Because – I didn't – feel like I could go to the wake. I was gonna, but. Your folks didn't – they always said to Eddie how I was 'loud'. And Eddie's friends . . . Eddie partied so much less when he was with me so they . . . I would have just gone in, fuck 'em, but – my face . . .

Ty   Right.

Dora   They don't – the doctors don't know what it's gonna look like yet . . .

Short pause.

Anyway, I just kept – all night, driving by the funeral home. His buddies outside smoking. Called information, got your number, left you that message, and just came here and . . . – What – was it – nice, or? . . . The wake, what was it like?

Ty   Actually . . . I didn't go.

Dora   You didn't go?

Ty   Same thing basically. Ed's friends, I can't stand those guys. And I guess Ed never told you, but I don't – I don't speak to my folks.

Dora   Oh. I didn't know that. Why not?

Ty   We just don't get along.

Dora   Uh-huh.

Pause.

I actually – I called you because – when I was driving by, like, the funeral home, I kept, I kept thinking about something you said. That night we all went out.

Ty   What?

Dora   That's the thing. It's like, I can't remember it! You talk so good – I can't talk that good. But it was something like – remember, Eddie was getting drinks, or in the bathroom or something, and you said – it was so loud and dark – in the bar – and I was like, Why, if you want to hang out with your friends, why would you come to a place like this? Where it's so loud you can't hear them and so dark you can't see them. – Do you remember what you said?

Ty   I think . . . I said that guys don't like to talk.

Dora   Yeah. But you kept going.

Ty   Well, that they go out because they're looking for a girl to sleep with or a guy to fight.

Dora   Yeah, no, it was after that.

Ty   Right – that they communicate with actions. Not words. Guys.

Dora   Yeah! That was it. That's so right, like. And it came back to me – because I was thinking – what you said, with Eddie. Like – what was it Eddie couldn't say. That he would do this.

Short pause.

That he'd – shoot himself.

Short pause.

Ty   I don't know. Ed was never the most – rational guy . . .

Dora   No . . .

Ty   Just – spending that one night with him. He was a mess.

Dora   Yeah. I actually broke up with him the next day.

Ty   You did?

Dora   You didn't know that?

Ty   No, I – no.

Dora   I didn't know if you talked to him in the time . . . between . . . then / and –

Ty   Right.

Dora   Did you?

Ty   What?

Dora   Talk to him at all or . . . ?

Ty   I – a few nights ago – he showed up at my apartment sort of – out of the blue . . .

Dora   What was . . . ?

Ty   Just. Um.

Well. Really, he seemed just – basically like he was fucked up on a lot of drugs. He didn't make much – sense . . .

Dora   That was it?

Ty   Yeah . . .

Dora   That fucking night. After you left. It was horrible. Eddie kept drinking, right. Then this guy Martin showed up, like three hours later than he was supposed to. Do you know this guy?

Ty   No.

Dora   Martin. Works at the casino, he's a bartender, and Eddie – thought he might help him get a job there, right? So we're talking and drinking and Eddie keeps, like, bringing up jobs and stuff, but Martin's not – he's not saying anything about jobs, right? Then Martin kinda leans in and says, 'Wanna know a secret?' And Eddie's like, 'Sure.' And Martin says, 'You know why you get so many free drinks in a casino?' And Eddie's like, 'Because the drunker you are, the more you'll gamble.' And Martin gets all quiet, like he's being all bad by telling us this, and says, 'No.' He says, 'We want, we give out free drinks because we want you to feel like everyone here is your friend.'

Pause.

'We do it so you'll associate the casino with getting something for free, with generosity. That's what makes you gamble more. We actually don't want you drunk, we actually pump oxygen into the casino to keep you sober and awake.' And Martin *laughs*. I think it's gross, this guy, talking about how they trick people into losing their money, but I look at Eddie – and Eddie's got this look on his face like – he's entranced. Like this is the coolest thing. But Eddie – I'm thinking, like – Eddie works hard. All his jobs, you can't fuck anyone over in those jobs, they can just fuck you. Eddie moves boxes. Eddie drives trucks, mows lawns, plows snow. Eddie gets fucked over all the time, so – why does he think this is all cool? Anyway, the night goes on – Martin doesn't say a *word* about any job. Takes out a bag of coke, Eddie's eyes go real big, like – that was it. Dragged him out of there, drove him home, puking in my car, put him in bed, and left.

Pause.

And . . . that was the last time I saw him. That night. Blacked out, puking all over himself. Called him the next day and dumped him.

Ty   I actually – sent him some money after that night.

Dora   You did?

Ty   Just to – I don't know what. Something . . .

Pause.

Dora   I told Eddie to invite you out that night. I wanted to meet you. He was kinda weird about it. He didn't talk about you a lot.

Ty   Didn't have much in common.

Dora   Eddie said you're like a genius.

Ty   He said that? That's funny. He never really understood what I do. It's pretty simple.

Dora   You work really hard though, right?

Ty   Not really.

Dora   Yeah, right.

Ty   No. I just have a skill most people don't.

Dora   What exactly do you do?

Ty   You really want to know?

Dora   Yeah.

Ty   It's pretty boring.

Dora   No, what *I* do is boring.

Ty (*laughs*)   I design educational programming for use in schools.

Dora   Uh-huh?

Ty   Which means – I take what would have been a schoolbook, and put it on a computer screen. So what I'm really doing is taking what something is – the content — and changing the look of it – the form – to fit a different medium.

Dora   Uh-huh . . .

Ty   I'm making it sound more complicated than it is. Like – all right: you have computers at Blockbuster, right? What do they do?

Dora   The computers. Just – keep track of your account. What you rented, if it's overdue, like that.

Ty   Exactly. Those are primitive programs – meaning they do simple tasks – but even so – think about before those computers. Someone would have had to write down all the information, what you rented, when it was due, and store it in a file cabinet, and retrieving that information would have taken time and slowed down the business . . . so, now, instead of lots of file cabinets and paper cuts and hand cramps, you have a computer on a desk and sore wrists and tired eyes. What I do is, instead of a kid sitting in a classroom, with ink all over his hands and seven books in his backpack, and five notebooks for his different classes – instead, he's tapping away at a computer. I'm sort of the bridge between the past and the future – or the file cabinet and the computer.

Dora   I have no idea what you just said.

Ty (*laughs*)   Meaning, we're not there yet. Kids still have books. They still write notes in notebooks with pens. But they won't always. Someday, they'll type notes onto a computer, and read lessons on a screen, and the teacher will type lessons during class, which they'll read on their screen, and be able to read when they go home, because they'll be doing their homework and going over their notes on their computers at home. I'm designing the programming that will make that happen.

Dora   Wow. What's the company's name that you work for?

Ty   Education Alternatives. 'Preparing Children for the Coming World.'

Dora   The backpack companies won't be happy. (*Laughs.*) I like my job. It's okay. People'll always wanna watch movies, I guess.

Dora *clutches her jaw.*

Ty   Are you okay?

Dora   The d-d-doctor said not to. T-t-talk too much. Nnnh.

Pause. She holds her jaw, in evident pain. Reaches into her purse, takes out a Vicodin pill, dry-swallows it.

I'm okay. Sometimes it throbs.

Ty   What?

Dora   The pain. It just, out of nowhere, this throbbing. I'm okay. I'm fine. – You had a horrible night, too, right.

Ty   What?

Dora   At the bar that night.

Ty   No!

Dora   Come on, you hated it.

Ty   No – it was really cool talking to you. I left because – I just couldn't watch him like that.

Dora   You were so uncomfortable like.

Ty   In the bar. Yeah – it's that thing – like Eddie's friends. I just don't fit in.

Dora   Eddie loved taking me out to bars. I hated it, but. He said he always wanted to show me off. I thought that was stupid, but. I don't know, is that how guys are?

Ty   Is that – are guys? . . .

Dora   Like, do you like showing off your girlfriends, or? . . .

Ty   Um . . . I don't – I never really thought about it . . .

Dora   Like, do you like to go to the movies with your girl, or do you like to hang at home?

Ty   I guess it – depends . . .

Dora   Yeah. Do you have a girlfriend now or . . . ?

Ty   No, no, not at the – . . . / no.

Dora   Oh – secret's out – Ty's a player!

Ty   Ha! / Right!

Dora   You are, for real. I see that little grin, that's a player grin.

Ty *laughs. Then clutches his stomach.*

Dora   Are you okay?

Ty   Oh, I'm fine, just – my stomach.

Dora   Is it? . . .

Ty   It's a – I'm fine.

Dora   That's funny. Eddie had stomach things all the time.

Ty   He did?

Dora   I always thought it was how much crap he ate. Do you eat, like, Burger King every day?

Ty   I'm a vegetarian.

Dora   That must suck.

Ty   No – it's really easy being a vegetarian. I cook / my own –

Dora   No, I meant, it must suck having people always assume because you have a twin, you're the same in all these ways.

Ty   Oh. Yeah. When I was a kid – I hated it. Everyone thought I liked what Eddie liked – because what Eddie liked was what everyone liked.

Dora   Is that why you got tattoos?

Pause.

To be different?

Ty   How do you – ?

Dora   Eddie told me. I hope it's okay that I – he was so proud, like – that you showed him your tattoos.

Ty   That's – he said that?

Dora   Could I see?

Pause.

They're – you can't see them on your / arms.

Ty   I wanted them to be private.

Dora   Right.

Ty   But. If you – . . .

Dora   It's just – I'm so curious.

Short pause. **Ty** *stands.* **Dora** *follows. A beat. Then* **Ty** *lifts his shirt over his head, covering his face.*

Dora   Oh my God. So many.

Short pause. She takes his T-shirt and lifts it the rest of the way off his head, and gently lets his T-shirt fall to the ground. **Ty** *smiles. She looks at his body.*

Dora   They're beautiful.

Ty   Thanks.

Dora   What do they mean?

Ty   They're j-just – abstract designs . . .

Dora   You're shivering.

Ty   A little / cold.

Dora   Did that hurt?

Ty   What?

Dora   The nipple ring?

Ty   Just – (*laughs*) just normal pain.

Dora   All down just the one side . . .

Ty   I wanted it to be ordered – not random, all / over.

Dora   He didn't tell me they were all down just the one side.

Ty   That's because – actually – he never saw them actually.

Short pause. She looks at him.

He knew that I had them, but I never showed them to him.

Short pause. She places her hand on his chest, slowly moves it down across his abdomen.

Dora   Where did you get them?

Ty   I – I did them myself.

Dora   Wait – *you* did them?

Ty   Yeah, I – bought the tools and studied and . . .

Pause. They look as if about to embrace; then, **Ty** *turns away.* **Dora** *looks out at the ocean.* **Ty** *reaches down to pick up his shirt.*

Dora   Wanna go swimming?

Ty   – Now?

Dora   You think I'm crazy?

Ty   It's – a little / cold.

Dora   You ever done it?

Ty   Swim – in the / ocean at –

Dora   At night?

Ty   No.

Dora   Eddie and I used to.

Short pause. She looks at him and smiles. Then she removes her clothes, to her undergarments.

Coming?

Ty   I . . .

Dora *smiles at* **Ty**, *then runs into the ocean, off.* **Ty** *watches her for a moment. Then he takes off his pants and rushes into the ocean, off.*

In the ocean, we see **Dora**; **Ty** *appears far behind her, slowly and blindly finding his way to her.*

Ty   OH!

Dora   TY?

Ty   IT'S COLD!

Dora   TY?

Ty   IT'S FREEZING!

Dora   CAN YOU SEE ME?

Ty   NO!

Dora   WHERE ARE YOU?

Ty   BACK HERE!

Dora   COME TO WHERE I AM! I'LL KEEP TALKING! FOLLOW THE SOUND!

Ty   OKAY!

Dora   HELLO HELLO HELLO! GOODBYE GOODBYE GOODBYE!

Ty   . . . GETTING CLOSER.

Dora   I HEAR YOU BETTER. HELLO HELLO HELLO!

Ty   HELLO HELLO HELLO!

Dora   SEAWEED! SEAWEED! SEASHELL! SEASHELL!

Ty   Seaweed! Seashell!

Dora   Ha! Hermit crab!

Ty   Hermit crab!

Dora   I think I see you!

Ty   Barely!

Dora   You're here.

Ty   Yeah – a hideous mistake but – here I am.

They are feet away from each other, though both looking somewhat past each other, as though still indistinct.

Dora   God it's so dark.

Ty   No moon. No stars.

Dora   There's clouds.

Ty   Are there clouds?

Dora   You can tell 'cuz the sky feels so low. Can you feel how low the sky is? Look up.

Ty (*looking up*)   It is low.

Dora   You can feel it, right?

Ty   It's colder than I thought.

Dora   It gets warmer.

Ty   Ha, does it?

Dora   You're really cold?

Ty   Shivering.

Dora   Come closer.

She moves somewhat blindly towards him, while he remains relatively still, groping a bit dumbly.

Am I – I'm right / in.

Ty   Yeah, I'm right / here.

Dora   Hold my hand to stay warm.

Ty   Hold your – where? – but I can't / see –

Dora   Find my hand, in the / water.

Ty   I can't / even –

Dora   Just move your hand around . . .

Beneath the water, both hands search. And connect.

There!

Ty   Yeah!

Dora   Found it.

Silence. The two look at each other, still significantly obscured by darkness so that though they are inches away from each other, they stare intensely as if far apart from the other. Their hands stay clutched.

Dora   Your face . . .

Ty   My face?

Dora   I can't see you . . .

Ty   I'm here . . .

Dora   You are . . . God.

Ty   What?

Dora   Just feel it.

Ty   What?

Dora *wraps her arm around* **Ty***'s waist, and moves behind him, clutching him. She sways with the gentle tide.*

Dora   There.

She presses against him, swaying; he begins to sway as well.

Do you feel it?

Now they are swaying in unison to the tide.

Ty   I think . . .

Dora   Close your eyes . . .

A beat. He does. The swaying grows more close, more intense, though it continues to be gentle.

Do you feel it? . . .

Ty   Mmm . . .

Dora   Right? . . .

Ty *opens his eyes. He turns his head to look at* **Dora***, whose eyes are closed. He stares at her a long while.*

Dora   Can I tell you something, Ty?

Ty *turns back, closes his eyes.*

Ty   – Sure.

Dora   It's a secret . . .

Ty   A – secret?

Dora   You don't have to say anything.

Ty   Wh-what?

Dora   A secret from that night at the bar . . .

Ty   What?

Dora   Shhh.

Dora, *eyes still closed, still clutching* **Ty**, *begins to kiss his neck. Again he opens his eyes and looks, as if about to speak. She continues to kiss him with great feeling. Then he closes his eyes and arches towards her. Their lips meet. Abruptly, he pulls away.* **Dora** *opens her eyes and looks at him. He stares back, somewhat inscrutable, as if about to speak but hesitant. Slowly their gaze entwines, and* **Ty** *turns away.*

She approaches him. She puts her hand on **Ty**'s *chest. He turns to her and with a sense of inevitability and deep communion they embrace. They kiss. Then* **Ty** *pulls back, ever so slightly.*

Ty (*whispers*)   I can't.

Dora   Shhh.

Ty   Dora.

She continues to kiss his neck.

I know, Dora.

Dora   Mmm . . .

She runs her hand up and down his chest, towards his groin.

Ty   Oh God –

She puts her hand beneath his boxer shorts.

Dora –

Dora   Mmmm . . .

She continues to kiss his neck.

Ty   I know – Dora – No – oh God – *oh* –

Ty *releases from* **Dora** *almost violently. Her eyes open.* **Ty** *strides back to shore, through the thick water.* **Dora** *watches him till he is off.*

On shore, **Ty** *dresses.*

In the ocean, **Dora** *stares blankly ahead. Then suddenly she plunges herself under the surface of the water, and hangs there, lifeless, peaceful.*

Just as suddenly she emerges, almost violently, from beneath the ocean. She sucks in air and chokes, then takes in a monstrous, gasping breath. Slowly her breathing normalizes, and she starts her way out of the vast dark ocean to shore.

On shore, **Ty** *sits, dressed, his head on his knees.*

Dora *comes onto the beach and moves to her clothes. Silently, she starts to dress.* **Ty** *picks up his head and watches her. She turns and sees.*

Dora (*conversationally*)   I do *not* wanna work tomorrow.

Ty   What time are you working?

Dora   Morning. The corporate people are sending all these people down – it's this thing they do after a robbery, this whole fucking interview thing. But since they didn't get any money it shouldn't be that bad, hopefully.

Ty   Right.

Dora   You should come in sometime. I got this stack of free rental coupons for dissatisfied customers, but we can use them for whatever.

Ty   Cool.

Dora   Someone was telling me . . . (*She's fully dressed.*) You can rent movies online now or something? Do you do that?

She looks to him. His head is bowed again.

Ty?

Ty *looks up to her. A beat.*

Dora   What's wrong?

Ty   I know it was Edward that – did this to your face, Dora.

Pause. **Dora** *chuckles.*

Dora   What are you talking about?

Ty   He came to me the night – he shot / himself.

Dora   You know – I gotta work tomorrow for like / twelve hours.

Ty   He told me he needed ten thousand dollars – he wouldn't say for what, / but he seemed really desperate – and –

Dora   He always needed money –

Ty   – he told me he was going to rob you.

Pause.

He was really high, he was fucked up, I knew I should have done something but I just – wrote him a check and – I . . . they didn't find it on him so. I guess – after he went to the Blockbuster he – that's when he decided to – that's when he came to the beach and killed himself.

Suddenly **Dora** *clutches her jaw.*

Dora   Nnnnh. Nnnnnh. Nnnnnh.

Ty *rises.* **Dora** *breathes. Then another wave of pain.*

Dora   Ahhhh. Ahhhhhhh.

Ty *moves towards* **Dora**.

Ty   Let me take you home –

Ty *reaches out to her.* **Dora** *slaps his arm away, her purse flung off her arm.* **Ty** *takes a shocked step back.*

Ty   What's wrong?

Dora *doesn't answer. She slowly removes her hand from her jaw. She gains her balance, then starts to move to where her purse is.* **Ty** *takes a few steps as if to retrieve it for her, but she shakes her head 'no'. She reaches her purse and, in agony, sits down. She takes out a pill. She manages to open her mouth ever so slightly; she bends her head back and drops the pill onto her tongue. She tries to swallow; gags badly; then forces it down.*

Ty *takes a step towards her. She looks at him. They stare at each other for a moment. Then she turns away from him and looks out at the* *ocean.* **Ty** *watches her for a moment, and then turns and leaves the beach, off.*

Dora *does not turn to see that he is gone.*

Scene Four

Day. **Dora** *approaches* **Ty**, *who is sitting on the beach. He is wearing headphones. So is she. She sees* **Ty** *and takes off her headphones.*

Dora   Ty.

He doesn't respond. She sees he's wearing headphones. She moves in front of him and smiles. He looks up. Eventually he sees her, and takes his headphones off.

Hey!

Ty   Hi!

Dora   Sorry I'm late. I would have called but I don't have your cell.

He rises.

Ty   It's okay.

Dora   What are you listening to?

Ty   Oh – just – a mix I burned – different stuff.

Dora   Trade for a second?

Ty   – Sure!

Dora   You're gonna hate this. Okay.

They sit down and switch headphones. Both sit and listen to each other's discs. **Dora** *rocks out a little.* **Ty** *laughs, grooves to* **Dora**'s *music.*

Dora   IT'S GOOD. WHAT IS IT?

Ty   IT'S THIS FRIEND OF MINE. CREATES IT ALL
HIMSELF, JUST HIM, A KEYBOARD AND A MAC.

Dora   COOL. – DO YOU HATE MINE?

Ty   WHAT'S THERE TO HATE ABOUT CYNDI
LAUPER?

Dora *laughs. They listen a few more seconds. Then* **Dora** *takes the
headphones off, and* **Ty** *follows. They hand them back to each other.*

Dora   Your friend is good. Is he from here?

Ty   Yeah, he's in school here. Doesn't go to class much,
spends all day writing songs on his computer. Big into
Ecstasy, kind of a drug freak.

Dora   Tell me about it. It took me so long to get off that
Vicodin.

Ty   Yeah?

Dora   Do you know you can get it on the Internet? My
last refill ran out and I was freaking, and then this guy was
like, I get Vicodin online. They have like online pharmacies
and doctors talk to you on the phone and stuff, and just
prescribe it. So then *he* got me some . . .

Ty   But you're – you're off them?

Dora   Yeah. I'm basically fine. I still have a little back
thing, but I do this water therapy, 'cuz the water helps it
supposedly.

Ty   Are you in a rehabilitation program or? . . .

Dora   No, they just showed me how, I do it on my own.

Ty   In the ocean?

Dora   It's too cold now. I've been using the pool at the
casino, actually.

Ty   Oh.

Dora   I went to this acupuncturist too for a while, for my back.

Ty   Oh yeah?

Dora   It really helped. They rake it in, those guys. Good line of business to be in. Everyone's back is a wreck, right? Nobody can walk in this country.

Ty   Or sleep.

Dora   Ambien for that. You like Ambien?

Ty   Never had it.

Dora   Ambien/Vicodin combo . . . like peanut butter and jelly.

Ty *laughs. Short pause.*

Ty   You look – amazing.

Dora   I do?

Ty   Like – nothing happened.

Dora   They did a good job, right? When they did the operation on my nose, they actually, I think they made it better than before. The girls at work are all like, Did you get a nose job?

Ty   Wow.

Dora   I swear to God. I thought the rest of my life, people were gonna look at me, like, 'What the fuck happened to her?' Like one of those people.

Ty   Right.

Dora   'Cuz I see those women. They come in to Blockbuster. Alone. The ugliest guy can come in, there's some woman with him. Ugly women, forget it. I got two new teeth too, see? Discolored, just like my real ones.

She bares her teeth.

Ty   Watch out, she can bite.

Short pause.

Dora   What about you?

Ty   What about me?

Dora   What's going on, player?!

Ty (*laughs*)   Not much.

Short pause.

I've – missed you.

Short pause.

Been thinking of quitting my job.

Dora   You're kidding.

Ty   Thinking about it.

Dora   Why?

Ty   I'm just tired of it. There must be something else I can do.

Dora   Don't quit your job.

Ty   No?

Dora   No. You have a good job, Ty.

Short pause.

Ty   Just something I'm thinking about.

Pause.

Dora   I'm going to this therapist.

Ty   Really?

Dora   Yeah. It's good, you know? We talk a lot about – we talk about everything that happened and.

Short pause.

Ty   It's okay.

Dora *smiles at* **Ty** *and looks away. Then* **Dora***'s cellphone rings. She checks it, then silences it. Pause.*

Dora   I'm sorry about that night, Ty. And not calling you and. I'm sorry.

Her cellphone rings again. She answers.

Hey. Yeah. I'm running late. At the store, we're rearranging the whole store and it's taking forever. No. Soon. Okay. (*Hanging up.*) Sorry. Meeting someone later . . .

Ty   It's okay.

Dora   The last thing I expected.

Ty   – What?

Dora   Remember that guy I told you about? Martin? Who works at the casino, Eddie's friend?

Ty   Yeah?

Dora   I guess he was all upset, like, that I wasn't at Eddie's wake, and so he called a couple days after to check on me. Turns out he's like this really cool guy . . .

Pause. **Ty** *looks away.*

Dora   My therapist thinks it's a really good thing for / me.

Ty   I'm sure it is.

Pause.

Dora   I'm not – I'm not gonna say some stupid thing to you that isn't true.

Pause.

I don't / want to –

Ty   I actually – have to get somewhere, so.

Dora   Oh.

Ty *rises.*

Dora   Can I get your cell?

Ty   Calling me at home is the best way / to –

Dora   Well – give it to me anyway.

Ty   Why?

Pause.

Dora   – I don't wanna say anything stupid to you, Ty.

Ty   So don't.

Pause.

Dora   – I want what I have to say to you to come out right.

Ty   Fine. Call me when you figure it out.

Ty *starts to go.* **Dora** *rises.*

Dora   You know that's not how I – wait, Ty.

He stops and turns.

Forget all that, okay? There's one / thing.

Ty   *Forget* it?

Dora   Just – there's something I need you to tell me.

Pause.

I need you to tell me the truth. 'Cuz I know you know it.

Ty   What?

Pause.

Dora   When I think about that night. I think about how you said you should have done something. How you should have done something but you just let him go.

Pause.

Sometimes I think about things *I* did to him. Things *I* said. And my therapist, she says, she always says, 'It's not your

fault that he killed himself. It's not your fault, Dora.'
But. Like. What *I* think is, Whose fault is it then?

Pause.

Because. In a way. It *is* my fault.

Pause.

Is it?

Dora and **Ty** *look at each other. Pause.* **Dora** *turns away from* **Ty**, *and looks out at the ocean.*

Ty *turns away, towards the shore.*

Then **Ty** *turns to* **Dora**. *He is quietly crying. He watches her looking out at the ocean. Then, as if sensing his eyes on her, she turns to him. A long silence. Then:*

Ty   (No).

Pause.

Dora   (Thank you).

Hold.

Where Do We Live

Where Do We Live was first performed at the Royal Court Jerwood Theatre Upstairs on 17 May 2002. The cast was as follows:

Dave/Young White Guy/	
Young White Man/	
Young Business Man 1	Nicholas Aaron
Shedrick	Noel Clarke
Billy/Young Business Man 2	
Art Student	Toby Dantzic
Stephen	Daniel Evans
Tyler	Adam Garcia
Timothy	Cyril Nri
Leo/Violinist	Ray Panthaki
Lily	Jemima Rooper
Patricia	Susannah Wise

Director Richard Wilson
Designer Julian McGowan
Lighting Designer Johanna Town
Sound Designer Paul Arditti
Composer Olly Fox

Characters

Stephen, *late twenties, white*
Patricia, *late twenties, white*
Tyler, *late twenties, white*
Billy, *late twenties, white*
Shed, *early twenties, black*
Timothy, *early forties, black*
Lily, *mid-twenties, white*
Dave, *late teens, white*
Leo, *mid-twenties, Asian*
Young White Guy, *mid-twenties, white*
Young White Man, *late twenties, white*
Young Businessman 1, *late twenties, white*
Young Businessman 2, *late twenties, white*
Security Guard, *early forties, black*
Violinist, *mid-twenties, Asian*
Young White Art Student, *mid-twenties, white*

Time

Late summer/fall 2001.

Place

New York City

Note

The play may be performed by nine actors. The actor who plays Dave may play Young White Guy, Young White Man and Young Businessman 1; the actor who plays Billy may play Young Businessman 2 and Young Art Student; the actor who plays Leo may play the Violinist; and the actor who plays Timothy may play the Security Guard.

I suspect the play's design should be simple and allow for seamless transitions; be indicative rather than representative. An insistent urban space with clear but weak boundaries, where different worlds press hard against each other, bleed through, blend and bend.

Scene One

Slide: August 9, 2001.

A bar. **Patricia** *works behind the bar.* **Stephen** *sits, with soda. Two* **Young Businessmen** *sit a few stools away, looking up at stock quotes on the television.* **Stephen** *is smoking.*

Stephen And he said, 'Ooh, you don't want to be a caretaker.'

Patricia Oh. Of course.

Stephen And I thought — I mean, the guy's missing a *leg,* what? . . .

Patricia Of course you did.

Stephen And he knew the facts.

Patricia What are the facts exactly?

Patricia *listens while filling pretzel bowls.*

Stephen Well. When I moved in, I just noticed – a family. There was a woman – and there was a man – and a kid – not a kid – maybe eighteen. So one day the woman disappears – I never see her again, and the father – when I see / him next –

Young Businessman 1 One more round here, Patricia.

Patricia *pours two whiskeys.*

Patricia (*nodding to TV, pouring drinks*) You guys losing money today?

Young Businessman 2 You're a loser if you're losing / money.

Young Businessman 1 You gotta be crazy to lose money in this market.

Young Businessman 2 (*nodding towards* **Stephen**) What's your boyfriend's name?

Patricia (*laughs, gives whiskeys to men*)   Here you go.

Patricia *goes back to* **Stephen**, *keeps refilling pretzel bowls.*

Patricia   So the woman disappears.

Stephen   – Right. And then, the man, the father, he has no leg suddenly. I see him, he has no leg below the knee.

Bar phone rings. **Patricia** *answers.*

Patricia   Hello?

Young Businessman 1 (*to* **Patricia**)   Ah, *that's* your boyfriend.

Young Businessman 2 (*to* **Stephen**)   She have a boyfriend? She never tells us.

Patricia   Okay. (*Hangs up.*)

Young Businessman 2   You ready to invest yet, Patricia?

Patricia   I'm already in the stock market – it goes up, I get good tips, if it goes down I know it's gonna be a bad day.

Young Businessman 1   You're lucky Bush got in.

Patricia   Right, yeah, thank God.

Young Businessman 1   More money for you!

Young Businessman 2   Three-hundred-dollar tax refund, what is that, how many tips is that? How many drinks you have to serve to get that?

Patricia *goes back to* **Stephen**. *The* **Businessmen** *laugh.*

Patricia   Okay, so.

Stephen   Anyway – I can't tell for sure but I think the kid, I think the kid is dealing drugs out of the apartment, because I see people go in there during the day – white people – so that's the / situation basically.

Young Businessman 1 (*re: the TV*)   Bingo. I told / you.

Young Businessman 2   Yeah, yeah, it'll drop, just /
watch.

Young Businessman 1   I don't / think so.

Stephen   Anyway – the father – knocks on my door
maybe once a week and asks me for cigarettes, and I give
him a few. This has never seemed to bother Tyler – *until* –

The phone rings. **Patricia** *answers it.*

Patricia   Hello?

Young Businessman 2 (*to* **Stephen**)   What do you do?

Stephen   I'm a writer.

Young Businessman 1   Oh yeah? A screenwriter?

Stephen   No, not a / screenwriter.

Young Businessman 2   You should write a story about
us. I'm / serious.

Young Businessman 1   Yeah, this guy's life is screwed
up, let me / tell you.

Young Businessman 2   – Two guys, one of them gets
laid all the time, the other one can't / get laid.

Stephen (*amiably*)   Maybe I will.

Patricia   Okay, gotcha.

She hangs up and goes to **Stephen**, *starts drying glasses.*

Sorry. This has never seemed to bother Tyler 'until' –

Stephen   – The other night. So the father knocks on my
door. He needs to go to the deli. It's raining outside and he's
afraid his crutches will slip. He tells me if he falls on his leg –
the amputated leg, the remaining part of it – he'll be in
really bad trouble. So I help him – I go with him – to the
deli. And as we're walking, he starts talking. Telling me he's
worked his whole life, he can't work anymore, he's on social
security . . . Anyway, so he buys his stuff, I help him back up

to his apartment – the end. And I tell Tyler this, I tell him this, and his response is – and this is his *instinctive* response – 'Oooh, be careful, you don't want to become a caretaker.'

Patricia   I see. (*Beat; sincerely.*) Do you love this person?

Stephen   Do I love him? Yeah – yeah. I do. I really / do.

Stephen's *cellphone rings. He checks the number, answers.*

Hey, sweets. Nothing, just stopped by to see Patricia. Yeah? Okay. Okay great. Bye. (*He hangs up.*)

Patricia   It's funny – because from what you've told me about him, he's been taken care of.

Stephen   What?

Patricia   Was that him by the way?

Stephen   Yeah.

Patricia   You told me that he has a trust fund. He's never had to worry about money.

Stephen   Right?

Patricia   He's been taken care of. So why was he threatened by your taking care of someone?

Stephen   Oh – right. Hunh. (*Beat.*) – It made me think about empathy.

Patricia *clears* **Stephen**'s *empty soda, wipes down the bar.*

Patricia   Uh-huh?

Stephen   Just – what it is. How it comes to be. On an individual level, a societal level . . . how do you imagine other people, their lives – whether it's someone you love or someone you don't – a stranger – I should get going, we're 'clubbing' tonight. – I guess it's really a small thing to get so worked up about.

Patricia   No it's not. (*Beat.*) I mean – the way you spoke of it, it doesn't sound like a small thing to you.

Pause.

Stephen (*lightly*)   Yeah. Okay. I'll see you soon. (*Puts down money for his soda.*)

Patricia   Shut up.

Stephen *laughs and takes his money back, goes, off.*

Young Businessman 1 (*to* **Patricia**)   Blah blah blah, *Jesus* that guy can talk. – Is he gay, that guy?

Patricia (*teasingly*)   What do you think?

Young Businessman 2 (*to* **1**)   I told you he was.

Young Businessman 1   He's a writer like you, / huh?

Young Businessman 2   – You know Patricia, there's this whole trend of attractive women hanging around gay guys, I saw a thing about it on TV.

Patricia (*laughing*)   Is that so? This is a trend now?

The men rise, take out money, preparing to go.

Young Businessman 2   Yeah, but it's not healthy, they're afraid of real men, they've been hurt too many times, so they take comfort in gay men. But it's bad, you're / cutting off from –

Young Businessman 1   Don't listen to this / guy, Patricia.

Young Businessman 2   What? It's just an / observation.

Patricia   I actually have a boyfriend, but thank you for your concern.

Young Businessman 2   You *do*. Truth is out. – That's a lucky guy. What's his name?

Patricia   Frank.

Young Businessman 2   What's he do?

Patricia   He's a chef.

Young Businessman 2   A chef? What kind of money do chefs make?

Young Businessman 1 (*he starts going*)   We'll get out of your hair, Patricia.

Patricia (*laughing*)   Take care, you guys.

Young Businessman 1   But I'm serious, Patricia, you'll be voting Republican by the time we're through with you.

Patricia   Yeah, right.

Young Businessman 2 (*going*)   Hey, whenever you're ready to invest some money, you talk to me first, okay?

Patricia   Gotcha.

Scene Two

Stephen's *apartment. R & B music plays.* **Stephen** *is dressing. A knock on his apartment door.* **Stephen** *turns down music and opens the door.*

Young White Man   Your elevator is *scary, yo!*

Stephen   Sorry?

Young White Man   Oh, fuck (*looks down hall*) – have the wrong apartment.

Stephen   Oh.

Young White Man   Sorry!

Stephen   That's okay.

He shuts the door. He begins dressing and singing and dancing as he does. There is another knock on the door. He goes to the peephole and looks in.)

Hello?

Shed's voice   Yeah, open up a minute?

Stephen   I'm sorry, who is it you're looking for?

Shed's voice   I'm your neighbor, 'cross the hall.

Pause. **Stephen** *opens.*

Stephen   Hi.

Shed   Hey, 'sup.

Stephen   Not much.

Shed   Yeah. Naw, 'cuz I know you help us out over there.

Stephen   Right?

Shed   Yeah. You know, I just wanna say, we appreciate that, you helping us out.

Stephen   Oh. It's not a problem.

Shed   But – you know – we okay, we take care of ourselves.

Stephen   Uh-huh.

Shed   You know how it is, we all live together, we all neighbors.

Stephen   Uh-huh.

Shed   Naw, 'cuz it's good to know, you know – everybody let everybody live their lives up here . . .

Stephen   Right.

Pause.

Shed   That's all. Peace.

Shed *extends his hand.* **Stephen** *takes it.* **Shed** *shakes, releases.*

Stephen   Bye.

Shed *goes.* **Stephen** *shuts the door.*

Scene Three

Shed's apartment. He enters, goes to couch where **Lily** *(who speaks with a British accent tinged with a black American urban sound) sits. They are sharing a joint.* **Shed** *resumes counting money;* **Lily** *is reading a movie magazine. The TV is on. There is a lock box on the table with cash and cocaine in it.*

Lily   What'd the faggot say?

Shed   Did I put the money in here?

Lily   What money?

Shed   Where'd I put the / fifty dollars? (*His cellphone rings. He looks at the number, answers.*) What. No. Not here. I told you. No. Peace. (*He hangs up.*)

Lily   Was that Dave?

Shed   No, it was the boys, looking to party.

Lily   That wasn't Dave?

Shed   I told them, find somewhere else. Keep calling . . . (*Reaches in back pocket, finds cash.*) There.

Lily   – What'd the faggot say?

Shed   He harmless.

Lily   Is Dave with Maryanne tonight?

Shed   – He fine, just spoke a minute. He not gonna call anybody, he scared.

Lily   Is Dave with Maryanne tonight?

Shed   I don't know, Lily.

Lily   What did I do?

Shed (*picking up cash, counting*)   – I gotta get that number from Dave.

Lily   What number?

Shed   He said, this one night we went to this hotel – he said he knew the guy who managed the bar in the hotel. You never went there with him?

Lily   No.

Shed   Amazing. I thought – way people spending money in / there.

Lily   Fucking Maryanne.

Shed   'Cuz I can't anymore – sitting here all day, never going outside, worrying about cops, people in the building knowing what's going on, calling the cops. In the hotel – watching people spend their money – so many people there, they gotta be / hiring people.

Lily   (*looking back at magazine*)   Do you like Nicole Kidman?

Shed   You know? Out of hand with this. (*Gesturing to* **Stephen***'s apartment.*) Like what if he called. What if he – what if he just called the police and said there's a kid in 6C dealing / drugs.

Lily   You just said he's harmless. Do you like Nicole Kidman?

Shed   Next time Dave comes I just gotta tell him, find someone else. But if he could set me up with / that hotel guy.

Lily   Dave likes you, he always talks about you, 'Shed Shed, Shed's my boy.'

Shed   That's why, you just gotta stop, you know, otherwise it keeps going.

Lily   You get paid crap. In hotels you get paid crap, they're all Mexicans / who aren't even –

Shed   Whatever, I got money saved now. Saved, so I don't need to – what I need. That's the thing, you just gotta stop thinking you can just keep / making more.

Lily   (*giggling*)   'Shed's my boy, my boy downtown.'

Shed   I fucking – I was a mover before. You know being a mover? Your back? In the summer? Fucking, people barking at you, elevators too small to fit all the heavy shit, people all freaking out you're gonna scratch their stuff, antique / whatever.

Lily   I have to see *Moulin Rouge* again.

Shed   How many times you gonna / see that movie?

Lily   Ewan McGregor . . . Do you think Nicole Kidman's pretty?

Shed (*continuing counting*)   She all right . . .

Lily   She's pretty, but do you think she's sexy?

Shed (*putting down cash*)   Five. – It's like, people too ambitious – like all that shit the boys talk – 'I'm gonna marry this girl.' 'I'm gonna get a recording contract.' Why don't you lay down one song first? Why don't you try fucking the bitch more than two months?

Lily   Me and Dave were together for three months. Maryanne thinks she / can just –

Shed   He fucked you for three months, you not together.

Lily   You've only known me one month, what do you know?

Shed   People don't – like – things happen for real, happen slow. People talking / shit.

Lily   Can I play a game?

Shed   Whatever, I don't care.

Lily *turns on video game, gets controller.* **Shed** *counts money.* **Timothy** *enters from back, using crutches.*

Timothy   Oh, you're not watching TV? I thought I heard the TV.

Lily *starts playing,* **Shed** *keeps counting, neither looks at him.* **Timothy** *goes, off.*

Shed   Five.

Lily   How many times you going to count the money, Jesus Christ?

Shed   Just making sure.

Lily   I can never get to the next level.

Shed   Just making sure he not skimming from me.

Lily   You keep it locked up, how's he gonna take any? I can't get to the next level.

Shed   Maybe he find the extra key. What else he do all day besides eat and fucking watch TV.

Lily   I don't know what I did.

Shed (*looking up to TV*)   You gotta press down *then* up. You don't do a double leap to get / to the gold rings.

Lily   No, Dave. I don't know what I did to Dave.

Shed   You didn't do nothing.

Lily   He's not calling me! Fuck.

She puts down controller, goes to couch, cuddles **Shed**.

Is it the same as the last twelve times you counted it?

Shed (*laughs*)   Yeah.

Lily *begins licking his neck.*

Shed   Lily.

She reaches for his crotch.

No.

He pushes her hand away.

Lily   'No.'

Shed   Nothing happening.

Lily   I don't believe you.

Shed   You know, no.

Lily (*moving to his chest, touching him*)   I just want to give you a blow job, what's the big / deal?

Shed   Stop, Lily.

She sits up.

Lily   You won't let me have a bump?

Shed   I'm done with that here, I told you.

Lily   One bump.

Shed   No.

Lily   'No.' Just one.

Timothy *enters, eating.*

Timothy   You done playing? You gonna watch TV?

Shed (*not looking at him*)   Why you be awake all hours, at night you supposed to sleep.

Timothy   I ran out of cigarettes.

Shed *calmly lights a cigarette and smokes.* **Timothy** *walks towards door.*

Shed   Now where you going?

Timothy   Get a cigarette 'cross the hall.

Shed   He not there, he left.

Timothy   How do you know?

Lily (*laughs*)   Shed knows everything.

Shed   I heard him go out.

Timothy   Maybe he came back, maybe he just went to the deli.

Shed   He not there.

Pause. **Timothy** *goes back to the bedroom, off.* **Shed** *goes to the door, looks out peephole.*

Shed   Giving him cigarettes and shit, giving him shit all the time – he need to mind his own fucking business. He thinks anytime he wants something he can just knock on the door. Prepared for nothing in his life, (*turning back to* **Lily**) now he can't fucking –

Shed *sees* **Lily** *has her cellphone out, is dialing, oblivious.*

Scene Four

A (relatively) quiet area of a club. **Stephen** *stands next to* **Leo**, *who is Asian. Pause.*

Leo   It's so over, isn't it?

Stephen   What?

Leo   All of it.

Stephen   Oh.

Leo   You didn't look like you were having a good time, so . . .

Stephen   I'm just looking for someone.

Leo   Who?

Stephen   I'm trying to find my boyfriend.

Leo   Oh, you lost him?

Stephen   I just got here – I can't find him.

Leo   Are you on anything?

Stephen   Sorry?

Leo   Are you on any drugs?

Stephen   No.

Leo　Drugs are kind of over, too, aren't they? What are we rebelling against except our own feelings?

Stephen　Good question.

Pause. **Stephen** *looks around.*

Leo　What's your boyfriend like?

Stephen　What does he look like?

Leo　No – what is he *like?*

Stephen　He's sweet, he's sensitive . . .

Leo　Do you love him?

Stephen　I do. (*Looking.*) There's so many people.

Leo　And the lights. And everyone looks the same.

Stephen　Uh-huh.

Leo　Or it's just that I look so different. What do you do?

Stephen　I'm a writer.

Leo　Cool – you're smart!

Stephen　I guess.

Leo　I'm in grad school – American studies. Whatever that is. Is your boyfriend white?

Stephen　He is.

Leo　I don't know why I keep coming here – I have no access. I'm totally ignored because I'm not blond and built and – it's like, it's so clear here, like – Who cares what we *do* in this world – it's all how you look. Who cares who *speaks* at our funeral. Just go to the gym and sign up, buy the right *clothes.*

Stephen　Uh-huh . . .

Leo　I look at this and it's like – how can you even believe in homophobia? Gay people are supposed to be oppressed but – come *on.* I mean, I believe in oppression – I believe, like, that Iraqis are oppressed and whole continents are oppressed in brutal ways – but *this*? – But I guess oppression is tricky, it's invisible now, more indirect, harder to define. Who do you blame if you can't tell who's oppressing you – you can't have a rally against invisible forces. And why would anyone here want to believe they're oppressed? It's not a pleasant way to live.

Stephen *looks around.* **Leo**'s *nose starts to bleed.*

Leo   I guess I'm talking mostly about myself. I guess I just wish I could disappear like everyone else here. Or maybe it's the opposite – maybe I just wish someone would look at me. I'd like to have someone who says he loves me looking for me! Maybe I should just join the gym and dye my hair blond.

Stephen *looks at* **Leo**.

Stephen   Oh – are you okay?

Leo   What?

Stephen   Your nose is bleeding, I think.

Leo (*touches his lip, feels blood*)   Oh fuck!

Leo *runs, off.* **Stephen** *sees* **Tyler**, *rushes towards him. The music is deafening.*

Tyler   OH – HEY!

Stephen   HI!

Tyler   YOU'RE HERE!

Stephen   I TRIED CALLING! I GUESS YOU COULDN'T HEAR YOUR PHONE!

Tyler   WHAT?

Stephen   NOTHING. YOU LOOK GREAT!

Tyler   THANK YOU, YOU TOO. SO – THE PLAN CHANGED A LITTLE. I WASN'T GOING TO – BUT I ENDED UP TAKING ECSTASY.

Stephen   OH.

Tyler   IT'S ACTUALLY BEEN TERRIBLE – NOT
THE ECSTASY BUT – LET ME FIND BILLY AND
TELL HIM I'M LEAVING. IS THAT OKAY?

Stephen   WHY ARE YOU HAVING A TERRIBLE
TIME?

Tyler   LET ME FIND BILLY.

Tyler *goes, off. A* **Young White Man** *comes to* **Stephen** *and
begins dancing, somewhat seductively, but with a ridiculous seriousness.*
Stephen *dances with him, politely, avoiding eye contact.* **Young
White Man** *demands to be seen, keeps dancing into* **Stephen***'s
vision.* **Stephen** *smiles and dances away from him.* **Young
White Man** *follows him.* **Stephen** *goes back to the quiet area of
the club.* **Young White Man** *dances away.* **Leo** *returns, holding
a napkin to his nose, pinching, checking.*

Leo   Thanks for telling me.

Stephen   Oh – yeah –

Leo   What do you write about? One of my areas of study
is queer representation.

Stephen   I actually can't really talk, I found my boyfriend,
so –

Leo   Oh, you found him?

Stephen (*sees* **Tyler**, *turns briefly back to* **Leo**)   Nice to meet
you.

Leo   You're going?

Stephen *goes back into the loud part of the club.*

Tyler   HEY – WHERE DID YOU GO?

Stephen   WHAT?

Tyler   WERE YOU TALKING TO SOMEONE?

Stephen   NO.

Tyler   WHO WAS THAT?

Stephen   NO ONE.

Tyler   SO – UM. THERE'S A PROBLEM.

Stephen   WHAT?

Tyler   WHAT?

Stephen   WHAT'S THE PROBLEM?

Tyler   WELL – WE JUST STARTED PEAKING? SO
BILLY'S LIKE, WHY AM I LEAVING NOW, WHEN
WE JUST STARTED PEAKING.

Stephen   COME TO THE QUIETER PART!

Tyler   WHAT?

Stephen *pulls him; they go to the quieter part of the club.* **Leo** *sits
some feet away, watching.*

Stephen   What's going on?

Tyler   It's kind of a long story.

Stephen   You said you're having a terrible time?

Tyler   Well, it's this whole thing. Michael's here, and you
met Michael, and his boyfriend Russell, and there are these
two guys, Keith and Derek, who you don't know I don't
think.

Stephen   Uh-huh?

Tyler   Anyway, so we were all dancing, me and Billy and
all six of us basically, and, Billy's had a crush on Keith for a
while. So basically Michael and Russell start dancing in
their own world, so it's me and Billy and Keith and Derek.
So I'm dancing with Derek because it's clear Billy wants to
dance with Keith. Then Derek starts dancing with some
random guy, and he disappears. So it's me and Billy and
Keith, and I don't, I don't mind dancing in my own world,
so I just drift away a little so Billy can dance with Keith.
Also we did some coke. Anyway. So I'm dancing in my own

world, but Keith keeps dancing towards me – but not just dancing towards me, he's doing this move, this really, like, provocative move, this kind of 'dance walk'?

Stephen   Uh-huh . . .

Tyler   Sort of . . . he'll dance-walk towards Billy, but at the last moment, at the moment he gets to Billy, it's kind of a diva move, just as he reaches Billy he turns away and dances back towards me. So he's going between me and Billy, but he's dancing more with me – he just, it's sort of like he's teasing Billy. And Billy says to him, he grabs him and says, 'Why won't you dance with me?' and Keith's like, 'What are you talking about?' So Billy tells him to fuck off. Just says fuck off. And Keith just ups and walks away. And I say, 'I guess it's just me and you,' and Billy says, 'No, it's you and *Stephen* and *fuck* you too.' And then I saw you –

Billy *enters.*

Billy   Hey.

Tyler *stands, moves to* **Billy***;* **Stephen** *hangs back.* **Leo** *looks at him.*

Tyler   Hey.

Billy   I can't believe you're going.

Tyler   I don't –

Billy   You don't make a plan for an evening and then bail out.

Tyler   Billy, you told me to –

Billy   Just stay, we made a plan. Come on.

Tyler   I just . . . Stephen doesn't want to stay, he doesn't really like clubs . . .

Young White Man *enters, sits next to* **Leo***.* **Leo** *hides his napkin.*

Leo   Hi!

Young White Man *nods.*

Billy   Fine. Go play boyfriend.

Tyler   *Billy* . . .

Billy   And this fucking E I got sucks.

Pause.

Tyler   Bye.

Tyler *goes back to* **Stephen**. **Billy** *stays where he is.* **Stephen** *rises and* **Tyler** *and* **Stephen** *go, off.* **Billy** *looks briefly at* **Leo**, *then makes sustained eye contact with* **Young White Man**. **Billy** *goes, off.* **Young White Man** *follows him, off.* **Leo** *watches, then looks around.*

Scene Five

Stephen *and* **Tyler** *enter the hall, moving to the apartment.*

Stephen (*playfully*)   I have something to show you.

Tyler   You do?

Stephen   Yeah, but you have to be a good boy.

He opens door; they kiss briefly before going inside.

Okay, sit down.

Tyler *pulls* **Stephen** *down to couch, starts fondling him.*

Tyler   I know what you have to show me.

Stephen (*laughing*)   No, stay here.

He goes off. **Tyler** *glances down at open book on couch.* **Stephen** *returns, sits down on couch, takes out pictures.*

Stephen   The weekend!

Tyler   Oh, you got them done! Yay!

They look at pictures, flipping through.

They were so nice. We should send that to them.

Stephen   – And there's everyone.

Tyler   – God, that house.

Stephen   – And the cat.

Tyler   Evil animal. – Oh, you took a picture of the cute boy.

Stephen (*laughing*)   You were the one who said he was cute!

Tyler   I did not – oh, *there's* a cute boy.

Stephen   Isn't that great! I love that picture of you.

Tyler   My eyes are puffy.

Stephen   No! (*Rising.*) I'm gonna put it in my frame, by the bed.

Tyler   Okay – hey, can I have the one of us that's in there?

Stephen   Sure.

Stephen *goes to his bedroom, off.* **Tyler** *picks up the open book.* **Stephen** *returns with picture and frame, sits.* **Tyler** *reads from the book:*

Tyler   'In the end, a whole vast area of Central Africa was completely transformed, not by the actions of some power or international organization.'

Stephen   It's such a good little book, this British historian Eric Hobsbawm . . .

Tyler (*reads with a bad posh British accent*)   'Everyone got involved: Paris, Washington, and the United Nations. Everyone tried to mediate and, I am told, there were as many as thirteen different mediators in Rwanda. However, it all proved to be inadequate.' (*He puts down the book.*) Did I tell you about this audition tomorrow?

Stephen   No. What's it for?

Tyler   This TV show? Want a massage?

Stephen   Sure!

Tyler *massages* **Stephen**.

Tyler   It's not terrible. It's about this kind of loser kid in a small town who learns he has special powers.

Stephen (*derisively*)   Special powers? Who are you auditioning for?

Tyler   The kind of loser kid in the small town who learns he has special powers.

Stephen *laughs.*

Tyler   Here, I worked on my special-power pose all day. What do you think?

Tyler *does special-power pose.*

Stephen   You're hired. (*Picks up book.*) Listen to this.

Tyler   I love you.

Stephen (*turns page, reads*)   'A Marxist interpretation / suggests –'

Tyler   I said I love you!

Stephen   I love you too! (*During following,* **Tyler** *resumes massaging* **Stephen**.) 'A Marxist interpretation suggests that, in having understood a particular historical stage is not permanent, human society is a successful structure because it is capable of change, and thus the present is not its point of arrival.'

Tyler (*mockingly*)   Marxist!

Stephen (*laughing*)   Interpretation, though. There's a difference.

Tyler   That *is* beautiful. You're tense.

Stephen   I am?

Tyler   Supertense.

Stephen   I guess I got a little freaked out tonight.

Tyler   What happened?

Stephen   It's not a big deal really.

Tyler   Am I hurting you?

Stephen (*laughing*)   I can't tell, I think you might be. Yeah, the – kid from across the hall knocked on my door.

Tyler   Why?

Stephen   Well, this other kid – this white kid – who I assume was here to buy drugs, but he went to the wrong apartment – knocked on my door. Anyway – he must have told this to the kid across the hall, and the kid – the black kid – must know I help out his dad or whatever, so he must think that maybe I know what's going on in there, and he just sort of wanted to let me know that he knew I knew what was going on – that he's dealing.

Pause.

Tyler   Did he threaten you?

Stephen   No, no. I'm sure he's harmless, but . . .

Tyler   Be careful, Stephen.

Stephen   No, I know.

Tyler   Okay, now me.

Stephen *massages* **Tyler**.

Tyler   I got a little freaked out tonight, too.

Stephen   Yeah?

Tyler   I was talking to some people at the club. I talked to this one kid who said he was sixteen? He said he was a pig bottom and was looking for someone to fuck him.

Stephen   Uh-huh.

Tyler   Oooh, right there. Yeah. I don't know, it started to depress me. The pig-bottom kid was so – beautiful and innocent-looking. How did he get like that, you know? – And did you see this? In the *Voice?*

Tyler *picks up* Village Voice *from coffee table.*

Stephen   'HIV Babies.'

Tyler   Rates are going up for people our age.

Stephen   God, that's unfathomable to me – that gay men are having unsafe / sex.

Tyler*'s cellphone rings. He checks it.*

Tyler   It's Billy. I'm not gonna answer it.

Stephen (*laughing*)   Billy calling to tell you to fuck off again?

Tyler   He probably met some guy and wants to ask me if he should go home with him. 'He's cute but he's not *hot, I* don't know, he has a nice *ass . . .*'

Stephen   Huh. Well – I'm sorry you got depressed.

Tyler   Yeah. (*Beat.*) Did you read your horoscope?

Stephen   No. Is it good?

Tyler (*laughing*)   Taurus, for far too long now you've been / waiting for –'

His cellphone rings again. He answers. **Stephen** *puts photo of* **Tyler** *in frame.*)

Tyler   Hello? Okay. Thank you. Okay. I have to go. I love you too.

He hangs up.

Billy apologizes. He wanted to tell me he loves me.

Stephen   Uh-huh . . . so . . . Billy really hates me, doesn't he?

Tyler   No – why do you say that?

Stephen   He's never very polite to me. He didn't even look at me at the / club.

Tyler   Part of that was the Ecstasy – we got our pills from different guys, I got mine from this guy Derek knew, but that guy didn't have that many, so Billy had to just sort of find his own and I don't think his were that good.

Stephen   He got the 'fuck off' Ecstasy.

Tyler   Billy's Billy. I've known him for so long, I guess I'm just used to him. He didn't have the easiest life, so he's sort of abrasive. You either get his world or you don't, is how he looks at it.

Pause.

Stephen   'Billy's Billy.'

Tyler   What?

Stephen   I don't know . . . I mean, someone says 'Fuck off' to you . . .

Tyler   It's hard for Billy – he doesn't have a boyfriend, his career isn't going well, sometimes people don't take him seriously because he's so campy . . .

Stephen   Well, you have to take yourself seriously.

Tyler   Like you, you silly goose! Mr Serious!

Stephen   Ha.

A knock on the door. Pause.

What time is it?

He gets up, goes to the door. **Tyler** *rises.*

Stephen   Hello?

Timothy's voice   Hey, I heard you were up, I'm sorry, do you have two cigarettes you could lend me?

Pause.

Tyler (*muted*)   Tell him you quit.

Pause. **Stephen** *opens the door.*

Timothy   Hi.

Stephen   Hey.

He gives him three cigarettes.

Here you go.

Timothy   Hey, you know, my check is late, you know? It was supposed to / come –

Stephen   Uh-huh?

Timothy   And I have to go to the hospital tomorrow, and the Medicaid is all – and my check is late – I'm trying to get, I'm trying to get this leg, keeps being delayed – if you got ten dollars, I pay you back when my check comes. Two days late now, nothing I can do . . .

Stephen   Sure.

Stephen *gives him ten dollars.*

Timothy   God bless you.

Timothy *goes.* **Stephen** *locks the door. Pause.*

Tyler   Ten dollars?

Stephen   – What?

Tyler   I just – that makes me worried.

Stephen   Worried about what?

Tyler   Just – that he'll think – you're a pushover.

Stephen   Right. But – his check hasn't come.

Tyler   You believe that?

Stephen   Yeah – I think it's pretty common, actually.
Social security, disability – I think the checks only come
once a month. It's a disaster for people when they don't
come on time.

Tyler   But if his son is dealing *drugs* . . . and *threatened* you
tonight . . .

Stephen   He didn't *threaten* me.

Tyler   You said you were freaked out.

Stephen   Yeah, but – I don't – think he would / actually –

Tyler   Like, what if they're working as a team or
something? Like, now they know you're scared, so they can
ask you for money and you're scared so you give it to them.

Stephen   I don't – think he and his son get along. His son
won't buy him cigarettes . . . I mean, if he comes tomorrow
and asks for ten more dollars, I won't give it to him, but . . .

Tyler   But what if they're, like, working as a team?

Pause. **Stephen** *looks away.*

Tyler   I don't know. I just worry. I get scared for you. I
love you and – a cigarette, okay. But ten dollars – and
taking him to the deli – you can't help everyone, people
have to take care of themselves.

Stephen   Well, you – you know, I mean – like – your trust
fund helps you, right?

Tyler   What – do you mean?

Stephen   You don't have to worry the way most people
do.

Tyler   But – I *do* stuff. My acting class, going to the gym,
preparing for auditions.

Stephen   I'm just saying – you know, he doesn't have any
protection. He's black, he's –

Tyler   But what I'm saying is, what if he just takes that money and buys alcohol?

Stephen   I'm sure he's not going to buy alcohol.

Tyler   You don't know that.

Stephen   Well, I mean, even if – I drink, we all – you're on drugs now.

Tyler   What does that have to do with anything?

Pause.

Stephen   Nothing, just . . . (*Beat.*) Like – talking to that kid in the club – made you sad. He – makes me sad. That he's in trouble the way he is, that makes me sad. So – I feel better helping him.

Tyler   Yeah, but I was in a club, I didn't – try to help him. I'm never going to see him again.

Stephen   Exactly. I – he's right across the hall. I see him every day.

Tyler   But you don't *know*.

Stephen   Know what?

Tyler   You have no idea what his life is really like, and I don't see how you / think you –

Stephen   There *are* facts.

Tyler   You don't know –

Stephen   – He has no leg.

Pause.

Tyler   I'm sorry. I just – I had a bad night. And I don't – want you to get taken advantage of. That's all. People with good hearts, they get hurt in this world. They do . . .

Stephen   I understand your concern . . . but – I think I'm okay here . . .

Pause. **Tyler** *moves to* **Stephen**. *He begins to nuzzle him.*

Tyler   Anyway, you should quit smoking . . . it's not good for you . . .

Stephen *smiles. They start kissing rather madly, and undress each other.*

Stephen   I love you.

Tyler   I love you so much, Stephen.

Stephen   Oh Tyler . . .

Scene Six

Timothy *struggles into his apartment, carrying a large brown paper bag in his mouth.* **Lily** *watches TV.* **Shed** *is asleep on the couch.* **Timothy** *shuts door, leans against wall, takes bag with hand, goes over to chair, sits.*

Timothy   He sleeping?

Lily   Yeah.

Timothy *takes a forty ounce of beer out of the bag, along with a pack of Newports and a candy bar.*

Timothy   Can I ask you, are you with Shed?

Lily   No. I was with Dave.

Timothy   Dave. You here, though, a lot.

Lily   Me and Shed are pals.

Timothy   Oh.

Lily   We're buddies! We're buds! I was with Dave.

Timothy   I don't know about Shed. Things getting quiet around here.

Lily   He's a big boy now.

Timothy   Yeah?

They laugh. **Timothy** *lights a cigarette, laughs.*

Where are the boys?

Lily   He doesn't want the boys here anymore.

Timothy   Why not?

Lily   He's a big boy, I'm telling you. No boys, no drugs.

Timothy   No weed?

Lily   No – weed. But no drugs. Can I have a cigarette?

Timothy   You don't got any?

Lily   Smoked them all.

Timothy *gives her a cigarette.*

Timothy   I used to drive trucks. Now I can't drive. I had a good / career.

Lily   I met Dave my first week here. We were together three months.

Timothy   Three months . . . I loved driving, get out of the / city.

Lily   Are you with anyone?

Timothy   I don't know, that might be over, all that. I got a photo album of me from before? Every time I would look at the pictures, I couldn't even / look at them.

Lily   Mm, I love Menthols.

Timothy   Yeah. – Did Shed tell you / about what –

Lily   Dave has this ex-girlfriend Maryanne who keeps manipulating him, ugh . . . So you're not with anyone?

Timothy   No – nobody wants to sleep with someone who has no leg.

Lily   Awww. Maybe there's a woman with no leg, too.

Timothy   I never seen a woman with one leg. Well, that's not true. But I wouldn't want a woman with one leg! Two things make people sleep with you is, you have a job, or you're young. I'm old with no job. I can't even look at the pictures of me / from before –

Lily   Do you jerk off at least?

Timothy   – I used to be a janitor before I was a truck driver. I can't do that either. Where are you from?

Lily   Chorleywood. Probably never heard of it. Fucking crap.

Timothy   Chorleywood?

Lily   Everyone knows everyone's business there, fucking crap. New York's different, has a different energy, do you know what I mean?

Timothy   Is he trying to get me out of here?

Pause.

Lily   I dunno. That's sad.

Timothy   I just can't – the social security went down, after a certain time, after I got out of the hospital, I get less now. But it's my name on the lease, he can't / do anything.

Lily   That's sad no one wants to sleep with you.

Timothy   Oh.

Lily   Does your dick work?

Timothy   Wh? – Yeah – it works, it wasn't damaged.

Lily   When's the last time a lady touched it?

Timothy   My wife.

Lily *goes over to* **Timothy** *and touches his crotch.*

Timothy   What are you? . . .

She unzips him, puts her hand inside, fondles him for some time.

Stop.

Lily   It's okay, you're getting hard.

Timothy   No.

Lily   There. That's nice. Is that nice?

Timothy   Y— yeah.

Lily (*still masturbating him*)   Yeah . . . that's nice . . . Does Shed have any other girls over?

Timothy   Used to . . .

Lily   Used to?

Timothy   Not so much now . . .

Lily *continues to masturbate him. He closes his eyes and begins to moan quietly.* **Lily**'*s cellphone rings. She stops, looks at the number, answers it.*

Lily   Hello? Hi, Dave. Nowhere, just hanging. Nothing. Where you at? (*Beat.*) Fuck her, she's a stupid cunt anyway. Okay!

She hangs up and gathers her things.

Timothy   You're going?

Lily *goes back to* **Timothy**, *puts her hand in his pants again.*

Lily   I bet you could come really fast for me.

She masturbates him for a while. He orgasms, stifling sound. She takes her hand out of his pants, wipes it on his pants, giggles.

I gotta go. See you later, sexy man!

Timothy   Bye . . .

Lily *goes, off. Door slams.* **Shed** *stirs a little.* **Timothy** *starts to cry. He zips up his pants, tucks in his shirt.* **Shed** *awakens.* **Timothy** *stops crying. He quickly lights a cigarette.* **Shed** *looks at* **Timothy**.

Shed   . . . You stealin' from me when I sleep?

Timothy   No, these aren't Camels. These are Newports. These are mine.

Shed   The faggot give 'em to you?

Timothy   I bought them.

Shed   Why you crying?

Timothy   I'm not. I was just thinking.

Shed   Where's Lily?

Timothy   She left.

Shed   She left? What, you scare her off?

Timothy   No.

Shed   When you gettin' your leg? Sick of this shit already.

Timothy   They keep saying next week! Then they say, there's some reason – you need to wait till the leg, you need to wait a certain time till it heals – they need me to practice, they have a leg there for me to practice but they say maybe next week – I can't tell – I think that it's not ready, the leg, but they don't say it's not ready, they say it needs / to heal before –

Shed   – Talking her ear off. You annoy people, you talk too much, you don't do anything, sit here, do nothing, fucking useless –

Timothy   What am I gonna do?

Pause.

Shed   Something besides annoy people make them leave / 'cuz you annoy them.

Timothy   No, Dave called. She went to Dave.

Pause. **Shed** *looks for a cigarette, his pack is empty.*

Timothy   I don't know why she likes Dave so much. But you don't know / with girls.

Shed   Fucking cigarettes, where's my pack?

Timothy   You all out? Want one?

Shed *keeps looking in empty packs, lifting things. He gets angry.*

Timothy   You want one? Here.

Shed *goes over to* **Timothy***, takes his pack away from him. He goes to the couch. He lights a cigarette. Pause.*

Timothy   Come on. Gimme back.

Shed *goes to the stereo, puts in a CD.*

Timothy   Shed. Gimme one, just to wake up to. One to go to sleep and one to / wake up to.

Over the stereo an Eminem-like rapper blasts. **Shed** *sits down on the couch.*

Eminem-like rapper
Don't give me no fag on the corner in the park
walking like a girl looking like a shark
trying to get at my balls
bitch get ready to fall
make a pass?
fag, I'll take that ass
empty it of gas
and put it in a cast
Shit, what time is it?
eleven o'clock
here, suck on this
no not my cock
boy, this a Glock

Timothy *rises. He goes, off, with his forty and his candy bar.*
Shed *moves to the song.*

Eminem-like rapper
all the faggots in the world today make me sick
it's a mystery to me why a man would like dick
'cuz I don't take that
no I don't take that

all the faggots in the world today make me mad
wanna make me happy? die and I'll be glad
'cuz I don't take that
no I don't take that
boy I ain't take that
who gon' take that

Lights rise on **Stephen** *and* **Tyler**. *They are making out, naked. They can clearly hear the song.* **Stephen** *stops.*

Tyler   What?

Stephen   This song.

Tyler   I know. – Don't worry about it.

The song continues. **Tyler** *kisses* **Stephen**, *they continue to make out.* **Shed** *rises, acting out the song, as if performing it.*

Eminem-like rapper
Damn, when I was six
growin' up in the proj-ix
with my bitch mom
every night she was gone
so my Uncle Rick'd babysit
and try to get in my shit
'Wanna play hide-and-seek?'
Uncle Rick, Uncle Rick, peeking at my little dick
man that's motherfucking sick
So suck
suck
No not on me
man, suck this blade
swallow your tongue
watch your faggot life fade
next I'm'a puncture your lung

Stephen *pulls away from* **Tyler**.

Stephen   I can't.

Tyler   Just block it out. I'm here. Think about me.

Stephen   I – I / just –

Tyler *leans in, kisses* **Stephen**. *He fellates* **Stephen**.

Eminem-like rapper
all the faggots in the world today love my shit
wanna get in my pants and suck on it
for real, gays love me and my song's number one
and if you don't believe me just ask Elton John!

Song continues. **Stephen** *orgasms.*

Stephen   Ohh! –

Scene Seven

Slide reads: August 14, 2001.

Stephen *and* **Patricia** *in a museum. In one corner, a black* **Security Guard** *crosses on and off. In another, a* **Violinist** *plays.* **Stephen** *and* **Patricia** *speak quietly, moving slowly across the stage. A* **Young White Art Student***, sloppily dressed, sketches, looking in* **Patricia***'s direction. He wears headphones and moves somewhat to their music.*

Patricia   It's good you're having a party. That's beautiful.

Stephen   It'll be a little hot, but I guess that's okay.

Patricia   Frank's gonna come, which is a miracle. – Isn't that beautiful?

Stephen   It's so chaotic. All that color.

Patricia   I don't understand this violinist – since when does art need music to go along / with it.

Stephen   I read about this, museum attendance is down, they did focus groups, people think museums are dull, so they're trying new things to attract more visitors.

Patricia   Great, next it'll be strippers holding up the paintings.

Stephen   That'll make Giuliani happy. (*Beat.*) Do you think people – do you think – how do you think people change?

Patricia   What's this about?

Stephen   Just a question.

Patricia   It's about Tyler.

Stephen   Well – yeah, but – generally, I mean . . .

Patricia   But there's a specific . . . ?

Stephen   We just – the other / night –

Patricia   Is that kid drawing us?

Stephen   What?

Patricia   That kid behind us.

Stephen *looks briefly at* **Young Art Student**, *who stops sketching when he does, then resumes sketching when* **Stephen** *turns away*.

Stephen   I think he is. – Yeah, it was just – Tyler and I got into it about my neighbor again the other night, he was upset that I gave him ten dollars.

Patricia   We should probably keep our voices down a little.

Stephen   Oh – yeah, I'm sorry.

Patricia (*moving to next painting*)   Mm-hmm? – What year is this?

Stephen   – I just, I wondered what I could have said to him to make him see my point more . . .

Patricia   Well – you know, you have to be gentle because – and patient. Think of where Tyler's coming from. You know, you dealt with your trauma by identifying with the pain of others, trying to understand it, in order to solve it. So maybe you're empathetic, but his history hasn't allowed him to develop – (*Looks back at* **Young Art Student**.) He is, he's drawing us.

Stephen (*derisively*)   I think I saw a Ralph Nader sticker on his bookbag.

Patricia   How rude is that. Who goes to a museum to draw people? Look at the paintings.

Stephen   Maybe you're inspiring him.

Patricia   Great, I'm glad I can be of service.

Patricia *moves to next painting.* **Violinist** *begins new song.* **Stephen** *follows, looking briefly at* **Young Art Student**.

Stephen   – But maybe I *should* have better tried to explain to Tyler why he thinks the way he does.

Patricia   Well – people have a lot to think about on their own without thinking about how they think.

Stephen   What do you mean?

Patricia   Maybe you have to learn to tolerate a certain amount of narcissism, you know? It's not easy to be alive and – all this, all these right and wrong ways to think – I think you should make room for just – who people are.

Stephen   But that's really scary, to think that way, it's so defeated. That's like / saying –

Patricia   – I need to sit, I have a headache.

Stephen   Art gives you headaches.

Patricia   It's not – talking and looking at paintings, it's a little / much.

Stephen   I'm sorry, I know I'm / babbling

Patricia   No, it's – you're asking valid questions, it's just . . .

They go to a bench. **Young Art Student** *gets up, moves behind them, continues sketching.*

I don't know. When I listen to you, I hear this – you're always looking for something that isn't there – something better – as opposed to reality. Who someone might be instead of who they are.

Stephen   Uh-huh? . . .

Patricia   I think you're setting yourself up when you look at things like that. – Okay, this has to stop.

Stephen   What?

Patricia *turns to the* **Young Art Student** *and stares at him directly.* **Stephen** *follows. The* **Young Art Student** *goes, off. The* **Security Guard** *laughs, crosses, off, as well.*

Patricia   How rude is that? Visual artists, my God. Voyeurs.

Stephen   Maybe he'll go home and create a masterpiece.

Patricia   Sometimes, this city, I wish I could be invisible.

Pause. The **Violinist** *begins a new song.*

Stephen   *I* see what you're saying. Like – his history – like, Tyler's dad was an alcoholic. So I guess you're right – it makes sense that he's so passive. When he was growing up, you know, nothing he did ever altered his dad's behavior. So he learned to protect himself by just cutting off . . . Did you know Tyler tried to kill himself? – Almost every gay man I know my age either tried to kill himself or fantasized about it.

Patricia   He tried to kill himself? Oh, that's awful.

Stephen   He drove his father's truck to a cliff, and he sat there, the engine idling, trying to get up the courage to drive over. When he was sixteen. He says he came so close . . . And I put myself there. I'm beside him. I'm with him at the edge of the cliff, passenger side.

Patricia   Empathy.

Stephen   Love.

Patricia   Mm. What's the difference, I wonder.

Pause.

Stephen   I hope people have fun at my party.

Patricia   I hope *you* have fun at your party.

They laugh.

Scene Eight

Slide reads: August 14, 2001.

Timothy's *apartment.* **Shed** *and* **Lily** *cuddle on the couch. The TV is on.* **Timothy** *enters. He sits down on the couch next to* **Shed** *and* **Lily**.

Timothy   What's this?

Neither answers.

 Ha! Oh, this show is a funny one.

Neither says anything. **Timothy** *looks briefly over at* **Lily**, *who does not return the look. He gets up and goes, off.* **Shed**'s *cellphone rings. He picks it up, looks at it.*

Shed (*a little alarmed*)   Dave.

Lily   Dave?

Shed *answers the phone.*

Shed   Hello? Yeah. Come up.

He hangs up.

Lily   Where is he?

Shed   He outside.

Lily   What should I do, stay here or go?

Shed   Up to you.

Lily   He won't go in back, will he?

Shed   No. He probably be here just a minute. He not gonna care – he gonna be like, 'Okay, you don't wanna deal, okay.' I'll give him his money and that's it. It'll be cool.

Lily   Is Maryanne with him?

Shed   I dunno. He gonna be up here, so go back.

Lily *gets up and goes in back, off. An insistent, manic knock on the door.* **Shed** *answers it.* **Dave** *enters. He speaks in an affected manner, often using black rhythm and emphasis without mimicking black pronunciation – his accent is that of a white upper-class person.*

Dave   What's up, dog!

Shed   What's up.

Dave *looks around.* **Shed** *shuts the door.*

Dave   Looking nice in here, looking neat! Where your boys at?

Shed   I told them, find some other place to party. Too crazy 'round here.

Dave   Lily said, Lily said. What's up, man!

Shed   Not much, not much, you.

Dave   Other than the bitches, everything is sweet – I'm *rolling* right now.

Shed   Yeah?

Dave   Three pills. *Good* Ecstasy, very clean, I met this guy, European motherfucker, shit's hot!

He flips through channels on TV.

Yeah, man, my mom wanted to have a *talk* tonight. Where can I *go*, like – the *re*hab talk. I couldn't deal, so I took three pills. Told her I had a headache, told her they were aspirin! She believed me!

Shed *(laughs)*   Aw.

Dave She's like, 'You're twenty.' She's like, 'I re*mem*ber
you. You were a *sweet* boy. You were *sensitive*. What
happened.' Truth, though – I was fucked *up*, dog! I was never
sweet. One thing I did, I never told anyone this – I started
rolling, and I remembered – I remembered I used to be able
– I could hear my parents *fucking*, and I was four*teen* maybe,
and I would go to the bedroom *door*, and I would – when
they were fucking, I would jack *off* – I would hear them – I
would hear my stepfather slap my mother's ass, or else it
was her slapping *his* ass – and I would jack off picturing it
and listening to it!

Shed Damn.

Dave 'Sensitive.' I would *come* on the *carpet* and I would
rub it into the carpet with my *foot*.

Shed Damn, why you do that?

Dave She's like, 'You were a good child.' She's like, 'Why
are all your friends *black*?'

Shed How she know that?

Dave Fuck, I have people *over* now. You gotta come over
and see this shit.

He sniffs cocaine.

'You've changed.' But nothing changed – that's what I'm
realizing, sitting there rolling.

Shed What you mean?

Dave I was *always* like this, I just didn't know what to *do*.
Like, why you do jack off when you hear your parents
fucking? – I tried to fuck the au *pair* when I was fifteen!

Shed What's that?

Dave Like, the *maid* – the black *maid*, I tried to *fuck* her.

Shed Oh.

Dave I didn't know what I was doing but. It was funny, I tried to *hug* her. I didn't know how to do it so I *hugged* her. Bitch hugged me back! I think I came right then!

Shed Damn.

Dave *hits a music video channel; we hear the Eminem-like song from earlier; it plays quietly throughout scene.* **Dave** *moves to the music, as does* **Shed**. *Then:*

Dave He's so over, don't you think?

Shed Oh yeah – he done.

Dave – Old Timmy here? Old man beating off back there?

Shed He here, he here.

Dave He's eating pepperoni?

Shed I don't know.

Dave Every time I see him, he's eating, I think, like, what, is he trying to grow a new leg? A new leg made of fat, like if he keeps eating he'll grow a new leg made of fat?

Shed Shit's fucked up, Medicaid, I don't know, keeps getting delayed, his new leg. He supposed to be getting it – on my fucking tit all the time, you know?

Dave – Things don't change, I'm telling you. Nothing changes, man. Nothing changes! – So I told my mom, listen, fuck *re*hab, I don't need *re*hab, give me the money you'd spend on rehab for me to make a movie and I'll stop doing drugs. Make a movie, right! Digital video – you can be in it! So she said if I write a script she'd do it. I'm like, You don't make movies with a script. You make it up as you go along. She didn't understand, though, she was all like, 'You need a script,' and I was like, 'No, you need a *con*cept.'

Shed Yeah. What – what would it be about?

Dave Me. Not *me*-me, but me, like, my life, you know?

Shed   Yeah. That's cool. Hey – um – remember we went to that hotel couple weeks ago?

Dave   Yeah.

Shed   Remember, you said – you knew that guy? That guy, he was like a manager in the bar?

Dave   Right.

Shed   I was wondering, like – maybe he could like, like if you could call him, like maybe they're / hiring people or –

Dave   Who are you sleeping with now?

Shed   Sleeping with? I don't know.

Dave   I'm manic, man, I apologize. Bump?

Shed   Naw, I'm okay. But / if –

Dave   I'm fucking manic. Have a bump, come on.

He smiles. Pause. **Shed** *does a bump of cocaine.*

There we go. – Damn it's good to see you. I wish I had some Es to throw you so you could be up with me. How long is it since we met, six months?

Shed   Yeah – since I met you in the club? – But that guy, like, remember / you said –

Dave   You see Lily lately?

Pause.

Shed   You know, here and there, that girl all over the place.

Dave   Jesus. Other night, I was fucking her and I was, like, Can I smack you a little? She was like, Yeah – and then she was like, You can smack me harder – Goddam, British girls, right? – So I started smacking her – she's grooving on that – she's saying it's turning her on more – so she's like, she tells me to smack her hard when I start to come. I was like, *hard*?

She was like, Yeah! She said it was the best she came in a long time!

Shed   Damn.

Dave   Unbelievable. And then she wanted me to fuck her in the ass – and the bitch wasn't clean! I was like, You want people to fuck you in the ass you best be clean, doll! – You have the cash?

Shed   – Yeah.

Shed *reaches into his pocket, takes out a wad of bills.* **Dave** *takes a long knife out of his backpack.*

Dave   Look at this, beautiful, right?

Shed   Wow.

Dave   I decided to start collecting knives.

He laughs, shrugs, and hands **Shed** *the knife.*

Antique, ivory handle, fucking gorgeous, right?

Shed   Wow.

Pause. **Dave** *takes the knife back from* **Shed**, *puts the knife in his bag.* **Shed** *holds out the cash to him.*

Dave   You know what? I had a good day.

He nods for **Shed** *to keep the money, rises.*

My mom went to the Hamptons, I'm gonna go home and party.

Shed (*still holding out money*)   What are you? – No, man, take / it.

Dave   Keep it, dog.

Dave *takes package of cocaine from the bag, gives it to* **Shed**, *who now has money in one hand, cocaine in the other.* **Dave** *slings his backpack over his shoulder.* **Shed** *rises.*

Shed   Yeah, I – I got some stuff coming up, I got to ask you about something.

Dave   – Damn, you got that hungry look in your eyes.

Shed   I do?

Dave   We need to find you some pussy, I think.

Shed   Ha, no, I'm all right.

Dave   Let's get you some pussy. When's the last time you fucked the shit out of a girl, for real?

Shed   I'm okay, take care of myself.

Dave   Dude – come to my house with me.

Shed   That's all right. But if we could / talk.

Dave   Timmy can take care of himself for a night! (*Yelling.*) Right, Timmy?

Shed   No, I should / stay.

Dave   You know I love you?

Pause. **Dave** *wipes a tear from his eye.* **Shed** *laughs it off.*

No – I don't just say that 'cuz I'm rolling. But, like, that we can be friends, from such different worlds. That's amazing. That didn't used to be the way it was. But it's that way now. People from different groups. People from different worlds. That's so beautiful – you know how special that is?

Shed   Yeah – I just. I – I never meant to get so deep in dealing.

Pause.

Dave   Oh. You want to *talk.* You're, like – taking stock of your / life.

Shed   Yeah, if we could / talk.

Dave   Bottle of wine, blow, talk all night – if you want to roll, call my European boy – we can sit out on the terrace.

You can see the whole city, look out, king of the world, for real!

Shed   I'd like to, but I / have to –

Dave   Let's call some girls and start putting an / itinerary together.

Dave *dials on his cellphone.*

Shed   No, I really can't, / man.

Dave   Fuck, let's call Lily!

Hits button on phone.

Shed   I would / but –

We hear a cellphone ring loudly. Short pause.

Dave   Shit, did I call you by mistake?

Shed *looks at the ringing cellphone.* **Dave** *looks at his.*

Dave   No, I called Lily.

Shed   – She's – she left her –

Dave   – Is she here? –

Shed   She – she's / napping or something.

Lily *enters.*

Lily   Hi, Dave.

Dave   What are you doing here?

Shed   No, yeah – Lily just hangin' . . .

Dave *looks at* **Shed**. *Pause.* **Shed** *braces himself. Then* **Dave** *laughs.*

Dave   Whatever. Lily, we're going up to my mom's, you gotta come. Who else can I call. Or should it just be us three?

Shed   I don't / think –

Lily   Where's Maryanne?

Dave   I don't know and I don't *wanna* know.

Lily   – You're rolling.

Dave   How'd you know?

Lily   You're so nice when you're rolling. Your face looks so sweet.

Dave   Let's move, everybody! Move move!

Dave *starts to go;* **Lily** *hangs back a second.*

Shed   – Naw, I gotta – I don't know, I gotta – I gotta make sure –

Lily *takes her cellphone and bag.*

Shed   I gotta – I gotta – hang out, I can't – maybe later, when he goes to sleep, but . . .

Pause.

Dave   Okay, call me later. Peace, brother.

Shed   Yeah, peace.

Lily   Bye!

Lily *and* **Dave** *go, off.* **Shed** *still holds the coke and cash.*

Scene Nine

Stephen's *bedroom. Party in progress outside the bedroom; each time the door opens, loud music and party sounds increase.* **Billy** *and* **Patricia** *are talking, both with drinks in their hand.*

Billy   But I have to admit, the rhymes are great, the music is really interesting – he's really hot – I don't agree with what he's saying, but he definitely represents what's already out there, he didn't cause it.

Patricia   Yeah. That's an interesting point.

Pause. Off, music is changed.

. . . So – how long have you been friends with Tyler?

Billy   Since college.

Patricia   Oh. Stephen and I met at college too. Where are you from?

Billy   Long Island.

Patricia   Oh. I'm from Queens.

Billy   Okay, can I confide in you? Can I make you my little confidante?

Patricia   What – what do you want to / tell me?

Billy (*hearing new music*)   – Oh God, this – who is putting this awful solemn *music* on?

Patricia   It's probably Frank, my boyfriend – he doesn't like parties, this is what he does, he fiddles with music. It's like he wants to make everyone as miserable as he is.

Billy   Well, *we* have the majority here. It's not 1993 and we are *not* in Seattle!

Patricia   I'll tell him to change it.

Billy   I want to *dance*. Do you dance, Patricia?

Patricia   I do.

Billy   Okay, go yell at your boyfriend and come back and I'll tell you my secret.

Patricia *laughs and goes, off.* **Stephen** *enters.*

Stephen   Oh. Was Patricia in here?

Billy   She just went out to change the music. Can I ask you a question?

Stephen   Sure.

Billy   Is there any cocaine here?

Stephen   Um – I haven't seen any.

Billy (*faux-sheepishly*)   Do you hate cocaine?

Stephen   Um – I don't make a point of it but – occasionally I do / like it.

Billy   I think this party could use some cocaine.

Stephen   Um. Let me look around.

Stephen *exits, off. Music off goes from rock to dance mix.*

Billy   Yes!

He starts to dance. **Tyler** *enters, dancing.*

Billy   There you are!

Tyler   Hi!

Patricia *enters.*

Billy   Patricia, I love this song!

Patricia   My boyfriend hates me now.

Billy *starts dancing with* **Patricia**. *The three dance.* **Stephen** *enters.*

Billy   Anything?

Stephen   What's Adderall? There are boys in there who say they have Adderall.

Patricia   Adderall? My eight-year-old niece is / on Adderall.

Billy   It's a prescription drug for attention deficit disorder, it's of the Ritalin family. Patricia, let's dance this song out there and I'll tell you my secret.

Patricia   Oh, right.

Tyler   Billy has a secret?

Billy   Not for long, of *course*!

Giggling, **Billy** *pulls* **Patricia** *into the other room, off.* **Stephen** *looks at* **Tyler**.

Stephen   Hey, you.

Tyler   'What's up, man.'

Stephen   'Not much, dude.'

Tyler   'Cool party.'

Stephen   'Thanks.'

Tyler   'What's your name?'

Stephen   'I'm Stephen.'

Tyler   'Hey, what's up, I'm Tyler.'

Stephen   'Would you like to dance, Tyler?'

Tyler   'Umm . . . I actually have to go home right now and wash my hair.'

Stephen   'Oh, right. Okay.'

Stephen *gets up and mock-walks away.* **Tyler** *mock-rises.*

Tyler   'But . . . I have time for one dance.'

Stephen *turns. They break the joke. They begin dancing.*

Tyler   So when everyone leaves tonight . . . can we take a bath together?

Stephen   Yes.

Tyler   Yay!

Stephen   I don't know how clean the tub / is.

Billy *enters.*

Billy   Patricia's boyfriend is *hot*!

Stephen *and* **Tyler** *turn and stop dancing.*

Stephen   Yeah, he's really / beautiful.

Tyler   Does anybody need a drink?

Stephen   I'm / fine.

Billy   No.

Tyler *goes. Pause.*

Stephen   So – um – I know, Tyler, you know, tells me you're a musical-theatre actor – what is it like for musical-theatre actors? It must be tough, there aren't that many roles for younger people, right?

Billy   Well, there's chorus.

Stephen   Right.

Billy   So . . . there's someone here that I've *slept* with – I think. Except I'm not sure he remembers me – also, *I* have a *wee* bit memory problem?

Stephen   Yeah?

Billy   It was a few years ago, I'm pretty sure it's him. He had, like – (*he measures out his hands*) – and I was like, um, hel-*lo*. Would you like me to *wrap* that for you? I think his name's Donald – such a bad name – but anyway, I sent Patricia on a mission to talk to him and find out his name.

Stephen   Wow.

Billy   So . . . I'd love to read your work.

Stephen   Really? Oh, sure.

Billy   Yeah, Tyler says it's so beautiful.

Stephen   Wow. Yeah, I'd be more / than happy –

Tyler *and* **Patricia** *enter,* **Tyler** *with drink.*

Billy   Patricia! Did you find out?

Patricia   His name is Philip.

Billy   Philip? Oh. – Does anyone want, I really want cocaine. Why does nobody have any here? It doesn't make / sense.

Stephen   I guess my friends / aren't –

Patricia   There's a lot of people I don't know / here.

Stephen   I / know.

Billy   Oh – what about that guy? Tyler, you were / telling me about some guy.

Patricia (*to* **Stephen**)   Do you have that book you mentioned?

Stephen   Oh, the / Hobsbawm? Yeah.

Tyler   What guy?

Patricia   I don't want to / forget it.

Billy   The guy in / the building, on the floor.

Stephen   Right, / yeah.

Tyler   Oh.

Billy (*to* **Stephen**)   Stephen, there's some guy in your building who sells cocaine. On your floor.

Stephen   Oh.

Pause.

Tyler   I never said it was / cocaine.

Stephen   Yeah, I don't know / what he –

Billy   Well, what else would it be?

Pause.

Why don't we do that?

Stephen   Um – I don't know if that's –

Billy   What apartment is he in?

Stephen   I think – I assume there's some system – I don't think you can just knock on the door.

Billy (*laughing*)   He knocks on your door all the time. What apartment is it?

Stephen   I don't – I think – I don't really feel comfortable, um – with his knowing that someone had come from this apartment . . .

Billy   But Tyler said you were, like, friends with him.

Tyler   I didn't say they were / friends.

Stephen   I basically have interactions with the father, / not –

Patricia   Maybe someone will show up with cocaine.

Pause.

Billy   What's amazing to me / is –

Tyler   I'm gonna pee.

Tyler *goes, off.*

Billy   What's amazing to me is that Tyler said they're also on *welfare?* That makes me, like, so angry. I had this actor friend whose father is a millionaire and who gave him money, but this kid, when his acting job ended, he went on unemployment, even though his father was sending him cash – I mean, how much money, if he's dealing drugs, / how much –

Stephen   No – I don't think the kid – the one who's dealing / drugs –

Tyler *returns.*

Tyler   People are having sex in your bathroom. They forgot to lock the door, I just / walked –

Billy   I'm sure they didn't forget, everyone in this city is an / exhibitionist.

Stephen   Who here would be having – I don't / like that.

Billy   Were they hot?

Tyler   I shut the door really quickly.

Stephen   Let me   knock on the door and hurry them up.

Stephen *goes, off. Pause.*

Patricia   I'm gonna check in with Frank.

Billy   He is *hot*, Patricia!

Patricia *smiles politely and goes, off.* **Billy** *dances.* **Tyler** *doesn't.*

Billy   What?

Tyler   Billy – now he knows I was talking about him.

Billy   Who?

Tyler   Stephen – that I was talking to you about his neighbor.

Billy   That you told me about his little project? His 'help the poor by handing out cigarettes' project?

Tyler   Can we just not bring it up again?

Billy   I'm sorry, I didn't mean to screw anything up. I just wanted some / blow.

Stephen *enters.*

Stephen   'The bathroom has been liberated by the forces of good.'

Tyler   Yay!

Tyler *exits, off. Pause.*

Stephen   So . . . the guy turned out to be not the guy, huh?

Billy   That's the thing – 'Donald', 'Philip'. That's sort of the same name, in a way, it might be him. I guess there's only one way to find out.

They laugh.

So . . . you've had a lot of contact with the drug dealer?

Beat.

Stephen   No – no, mostly with his father.

Billy   The crippled guy.

Stephen   Yeah, the – disabled guy, right. Yeah, and – it's not – I'm not sure how much Tyler told you but – it's not the kid who's on welfare. He's not collecting money – it's / the father.

Tyler *enters.*

Tyler   Now someone else is in there and I knocked and they were like, 'It's gonna take a while.'

Billy   But that's so sick, though.

Stephen   What is?

Billy   That on top of the drug money they're collecting / welfare.

Stephen   No – I don't think the son gives the father any money – is what I'm saying.

Tyler *looks away.*

Billy (*to* **Tyler**)   Stephen was just telling me some more about the neighbors.

Tyler   Oh.

Stephen   Just – I think it's / complicated.

Patricia *enters.*

Billy   Well, thank God that welfare bill passed so that kind of stuff can't happen as much anymore, thank God.

Patricia   – Those boys doing Adderall are nuts, they asked me if I wanted to play strip poker.

Tyler   Really? Oh God –

Stephen (*to* **Billy**)   – No. No actually. The welfare bill – in this – in this building alone – in apartments no bigger than this one, there are people – families of *ten* living together, three generations.

Stephen *looks to* **Patricia**.

Billy   Well, that's what they get, though. They had five years to get off welfare and find / jobs.

Stephen   Are you – do you actually know about the welfare / bill?

Tyler   – Stephen.

Billy   Actually, I / do.

Tyler   Stephen –

Stephen   What?

Billy   I grew up poor.

Stephen *looks back to* **Billy**.

Stephen   Right. But – the welfare / bill –

Billy   And we never went on welfare. My father worked two jobs.

Stephen   I hear that, definitely. And I'm speaking from an upper-middle-class perspective, / but –

Billy   I mean, my father and my mother – that was all they did – was work. No / one –

Stephen   Right. – Okay. But – the welfare bill is actually – a really terrible – you know, the effects are not always visible, they're never immediately apparent, and it's coincided with a bright time for what's really a very fragile / economy –

Billy   But it made the poor take responsibility for themselves.

Stephen   Well – it terrorized them – I don't know how you can say / it –

Tyler   Stephen.

Billy   You have to admit how much better this city is now.

Stephen   But – what do you mean 'better', I / don't –

Billy (*to* **Tyler** *and* **Patricia**)   This city is *so* much better than it was even five years ago.

Stephen   Okay – do you really want to have a conversation about this?

Billy (*to* **Stephen**)   There's less homeless, / there's –

Stephen   You *see* them less – where *you* live –

Billy   – it put a stop to all those welfare mothers who kept having / babies –

Stephen   Welfare – do you – *welfare* / mothers?

Tyler   Stephen.

Stephen   – Why do you keep saying my name?

Tyler   Just . . .

Stephen *turns to* **Billy**.

Stephen   I'd like to talk to you about this but – we're sort of talking around each other.

Pause.

Billy   I guess it's that – you know, my mother and father worked so hard for me. They gave up their lives for me. No one handed them anything.

Stephen   Right.

Billy   You know?

Stephen   Sure. But – did you ever think that it was easier for them because they're white?

Billy   Well – they faced anti-Semitism all their lives . . .

Stephen   Right. But – being Jewish is very different from being black.

Billy Whoa.

Pause.

Stephen What?

Billy You don't know my life.

Stephen I didn't say I did.

Billy Yes, you're talking about my life – 'it was easier for them because they were white' –

Stephen Well – I'm – talking about facts of history, facts of race, facts / of –

Billy You don't know my life or their / lives.

Stephen I didn't say / I knew –

Billy My mother is dead.

Pause. **Patricia** *takes her drink glass and exits.*

Stephen We're not talking about that.

Pause. **Billy** *moves to leave the room.*

Stephen No – I mean – of course – I'm sure your parents did work hard, I'm sure they encountered anti-Semitism. But – there are not jobs for everyone, particularly not for people who don't speak English well, who weren't given access to a good education, or, I mean – in terms of comparing – you can't really argue that Jews have had anywhere *near* the experience that blacks have had / in America.

Billy You don't know their / lives, Jesus.

Stephen I'm – no, listen – just – stop being so defensive and listen a / second.

Billy I / am.

Stephen A culture of poverty and racism breeds a – I mean, can't you, as a gay man, I mean, can't you identify with other / groups?

Billy   You just can't expect the world to give you things, that's all I'm saying. No one ever gave me anything. And say what you will about Giuliani, fuck him for shutting down the clubs and all that, and fuck him for trying to censor art, but he cleaned this city up.

Pause.

Stephen   It's apartment 6C.

Billy   What is?

Tyler   Stephen.

Stephen   If you want to buy drugs. Apartment 6C.

Pause. **Billy** *looks at* **Tyler**. **Billy** *goes, off. Pause.* **Stephen** *looks at* **Tyler**, *who looks at the floor.*

Stephen   What? Let him go – let him get punched in the face – fucking privilege, fucking – I'm sorry, Tyler, if someone is going to stand in my apartment and say / racist –

Patricia *enters.*

Patricia   Hey.

Stephen   Hey.

Patricia   So, Frank wants to go home, I have a lot of work to catch up on, so . . .

Stephen   Oh.

Patricia   I'll talk to you tomorrow. Bye, Tyler.

Tyler   Bye, Patricia.

Patricia *goes, off. Pause.*

Tyler (*quietly*)   You should let people have their opinions, Stephen.

Stephen   Not – not when they're racist and / wrong.

Tyler   It's not racist to think welfare is bad, or, or, that all the problems of the world won't be solved if the government gives poor people more money.

Stephen   Tyler, people are / dying.

Tyler   I just want you two to get / along.

Stephen   People are dying in this building. They are dying of poverty, of drugs, I see them every day, there are no jobs, I see their children, they go to schools that are falling apart.

Tyler   Not all of them.

Stephen   Well – some of them.

Tyler *goes to* **Stephen** *and puts his hand on his shoulder.*

Tyler   Fine, but why does it upset you so much?

Stephen   – I *live* here!

Tyler   Whoa! Calm down.

He hugs **Stephen**.

Shhhh.

They begin dancing slowly. Lights rise on **Timothy**'s *apartment.* **Shed** *stands, holding the cocaine and the cash.* **Billy** *knocks on his door. Pause.* **Shed** *goes to the door, looks in the peephole. He puts the money and the cocaine in his pockets and opens the door.*

Billy   Hey . . . I'm from across the hall? At the party?

He takes out forty dollars.

I have forty dollars. Do you have any coke?

Pause. **Shed** *looks at him. He lets go of the door.* **Billy** *holds the door open, steps inside.* **Shed** *turns around. He takes the forty dollars from* **Billy**, *gets cocaine, gives it to* **Billy**.

Billy   Thanks.

Billy *goes, off.* **Timothy** *enters.*

Timothy   Who was that.

Shed *doesn't answer.*

Timothy   Where's Lily? She go?

Shed   Yeah.

Timothy   She go with Dave?

Shed   You a fucking eavesdropper now?

Timothy   Don't worry about that – she's crazy, Shed –

Shed   – I don't care about that –

Timothy   – Don't pay her no mind –

Shed   – Leave me alone –

Timothy   – I'm just saying – she tried to grab my dick once – she's crazy, she / just –

Shed *rushes* **Timothy** *and throws him against the wall. He punches him in the shoulder.* **Timothy** *falls.*

Timothy (*crying out*)   Ahhh! My leg!

Shed *sits down on the couch and turns on the television.* **Timothy** *whimpers in pain.* **Billy** *enters the bedroom, where* **Stephen** *and* **Tyler** *dance.*

Billy   Can we make up, Stephen?

Stephen *looks at* **Billy**.

In **Timothy**'s *apartment.*

Shed   Here all the time – in people's shit all the time – can't do nothing yourself –

Timothy *just lies there.*

Stephen   Yeah, I don't – I didn't want to fight.

Shed   – You gonna just lay there now?

Billy   Me too. I'm sorry if what I said offended you.

Shed – Get up!

Stephen   Don't worry about it.

Shed Get up!

Billy   Okay.

Shed *begins playing video game.* **Timothy** *reaches out for crutches. He can't reach.*

Billy   Could you apologize to me too?

Stephen – Excuse me?

Tyler *turns away.*

Billy   For assuming you knew about my life.

Shed *kicks crutch over to* **Timothy***, who can now reach it, returns to couch and plays game.*

Stephen   Okay, I just. I think it's important that people – think about – other people, you know. Think about / what they –

Billy*'s cellphone rings. He checks it but does not answer. Pause.* **Stephen** *looks at* **Tyler***.*

Stephen *(flippantly)*   I apologize.

Billy   I accept. Now we can party? Tyler loves you, I want us to get along. He loves both of us so we should try to at least like each other.

Stephen – Right.

Pause.

Billy *(singsongy)*   I got *blo-ow!*

Billy *takes out cocaine. He scoops some onto a key and sniffs it. He offers it to* **Tyler***.*

Tyler   A little . . .

Tyler *sniffs cocaine.* **Billy** *offers it to* **Stephen***. Pause.*

Stephen   I'm okay.

Billy   You sure?

Stephen   Yeah, I'm fine.

Billy   It's good, I think.

Billy *puts away the cocaine. Pause.*

Tyler   I'm gonna see if I can pee again.

Tyler *goes, off. In* **Timothy***'s apartment,* **Timothy** *finally rises, in pain.* **Shed** *continues to play video game.*

Billy   So . . . what are you writing these days?

Timothy *begins to exit.* **Stephen** *doesn't respond, as if lost in thought.*

Billy   Oh, don't worry – that's just Tyler being Tyler. He'll be fine, he doesn't like conflict.

Stephen   Why did you do that?

Billy   Do what?

A new song comes on, off. A sound of cheering from the party.

Stephen   You – you brought up – you created / a –

Billy *(starting to dance)*   – I love this song –

Stephen   – Fuck off.

Billy   What? – What is wrong with you?

Pause. **Billy** *goes, off. In* **Timothy***'s apartment,* **Timothy** *exits, off.* **Shed** *looks back, then turns back to video game. In* **Stephen***'s apartment,* **Tyler** *bounces into the bedroom, dancing.*

Stephen   Hey.

Tyler   What's up, man. The tub is clean . . .

Stephen *smiles.*

Tyler   Let's dance.

He grabs **Stephen***, tries to dance.* **Stephen** *doesn't dance.*

Tyler   Or not.

Stephen   I'm – just . . .

Tyler   Billy's fine, don't worry about it. Come on, dance.

Stephen *dances with* **Tyler** *tentatively. Then stops again.*

Stephen   I don't – it's – *I'm* upset.

Tyler   You're upset.

Stephen   Yeah, I – I'm really sad now.

Pause. **Tyler** *places his hands on* **Stephen***'s head, and begins making a strange humming sound.* **Stephen** *laughs a little.*

Stephen   What are you? . . .

Tyler   'I'm using my special powers to take away your pain.' Hmmmmmmmzzz.

Stephen   Oh.

Tyler   I have a call-back!

Stephen   For the TV show?

Tyler   Hmmmmmmzzz.

Stephen *pushes* **Tyler***'s hands off him.*

Tyler   What.

Stephen   I'm – really sad, Tyler.

Tyler   It's a *party*, Stephen.

Stephen   I know it's –

Tyler (*taking* **Stephen***'s hand*)   Let's go out to the party, come / on.

Stephen   In – a minute.

Long pause. **Stephen** *and* **Tyler** *look at each other.*

Tyler   Fine.

Tyler *goes, off.* **Stephen** *stays on his bed.* **Shed** *continues to play the video game, with growing intensity.*

Scene Ten

Slide reads: August 15, 2001.

Stephen *and* **Patricia** *sit in* **Stephen***'s living room.*

Patricia   I always wondered why gay men had all these friends in the way they do. It's so clear. It's so they can separate their sexual and emotional needs, because they're frightened to combine them. Boyfriends who don't have sex, sex without having to have a boyfriend.

Stephen   Yeah . . . I dunno. Maybe he'll – maybe he'll change his mind. Just – like that. I just . . .

Patricia   I'm really sorry.

Pause.

I should get to work. Did you have that book? . . .

Stephen   Oh, right.

Stephen *gets book, gives it to* **Patricia***. She looks at it.*

Patricia   *On the Edge of the New Century.* There's a title for you.

Stephen   It's really great.

Patricia *rises;* **Stephen** *follows. She moves to the door.*

Patricia   You know, anyone who's friends with that guy – 'Billy' – all he would talk to me about was how attractive Frank was. And about – whoever this guy was he thought he had had sex with. He was actually why we left.

Stephen   Billy?

Patricia   Yeah.

Stephen   But you said you left because Frank wanted to go. Because you had work to do.

Pause.

Patricia   Yeah – I mean – we were just being polite. (*Laughs.*) I felt like I was at work – except instead of a straight guy telling me how attractive I am, it was a gay man telling me how attractive my boyfriend is.

Stephen   Why were you being polite? You weren't at work.

Pause.

Patricia   What do you mean?

Stephen   I thought you left because of Frank – but you're saying you were offended by Billy.

Patricia   Yeah.

Stephen   But you didn't say anything.

Patricia   About what?

Pause.

Stephen   I'm sorry, I'm just . . . I'm really angry.

Patricia   Well – of course you're angry. Tyler said he loved you. He was supposed to love you. He didn't love / you.

Stephen   No. Not that.

Patricia   What?

Stephen   You know – You're talking about how you left and. You know, I – I had no support. No one . . .

Pause.

Patricia   I see. I think – you're talking about the discussion about / welfare.

Stephen   Yes, when you left. Because I was thinking – I knew that you agreed with me. I knew that, and now you're saying on top of that you were offended by Billy but you just –

Patricia   Right. Okay. What I was thinking was, was that nobody's mind was going to be changed. Clearly. And it was a ridiculous conversation to be having.

Stephen   It wasn't a ridiculous conversation to be having.

Patricia   No – but at a party. And that guy wasn't going to budge an / inch.

Stephen   But – you know, maybe if you had spoken up – maybe he could have been made to listen.

Patricia   That never would have happened. (*Beat.*) Billy – what I was thinking, was – when you grow up poor, it's very painful to think of yourself as being like other poor people. I know what it's like to be / defensive about –

Stephen   But you're not seeing how – how I was made to look like a jerk, while Billy gets to – and in front of Tyler, you know, I seem like the asshole.

Pause.

Patricia   I see now. You're feeling that maybe Tyler left you because of this conversation about welfare?

Stephen   Where I looked like an / asshole.

Patricia   Right, but – I think the timing's fortuitous. I don't think it makes sense to say that this one moment – what did he say? 'Different places' – 'need to be alone' – clichés, they mean nothing. So of course you're searching for why, and it was at that moment that you felt Tyler pull away, but . . . But it's not just – it's not – Here's what I think happened in that moment – because it was more than just that moment, I mean: you were angry at Tyler for validating Billy because you found Billy offensive, because of how he looked at the world. And you wanted Tyler to look at the world like you do. You could sense that Billy was engaging you in a way meant to humiliate you and test loyalties and yet you couldn't censor / yourself.

Stephen   But now you are implying a psychodrama. You are implying that politics isn't real, that a political discussion is merely a psychodrama. As if what we were talking about isn't valid – as if it's something / else.

Patricia   That's not, / no –

Stephen   Which allows you to leave. To pretend it's something else and to leave, so I'm left there. The way I look at the world, alone, unsupported, ridiculous, when I know / you –

Patricia   You're making this too easy, Stephen.

Stephen   No. That's what you did. You made it easy for yourself and easy for Billy, you left. You were invisible. You made yourself invisible.

Patricia   Okay . . . you're – very angry at me.

Stephen   I – am. Yeah. Yeah, if you had supported me, Tyler might have seen that I wasn't – Billy might have listened and Tyler would have – fuck it, whatever. You can go.

Patricia   Well – now I don't want to go.

Stephen   Well I want you to.

Pause. **Patricia** *moves to the door.*

Stephen   No one's mind can be changed. This is the world.

Patricia *stops, turns.*

Patricia   Would you like me to go?

Stephen   Let everyone have their own opinions, everyone's opinion is equal, everyone / is valid.

Patricia   Maybe you need to change the way you talk to people who don't agree with you. Maybe that's what Tyler saw – that you / weren't . . .

Stephen   Oh?

Patricia   Yeah. Maybe you need to change the way you talk to people you feel superior / to.

Stephen   Blah blah blah. Just go.

Pause. **Patricia** *goes to the table, places the book down, and leaves, off. Pause.* **Stephen** *lights a cigarette. A knock on the door.*

Stephen (*calls*)   Hello?

Timothy's voice   Hey, sorry to bother you, you got a cigarette?

Pause.

Stephen   I quit.

Timothy's voice   What's that?

Stephen   I QUIT.

Scene Eleven

Slide reads: September 27, 2001.

Timothy's *apartment.* **Lily** *sits alone, flipping through a photo album.* **Timothy**, *with prosthetic leg, enters from back, walking slowly.*

Timothy   He not back yet?

Lily   No.

Timothy   Usually back by now.

Timothy *starts to walk, off.*

Lily   How long have you lived here?

Timothy *turns. He sees she is looking at the photo album.*

Timothy   Oh, you looking at the pictures?

She nods.

Ten years. Yeah. Moved in when we got married.

Lily   Ten years. Wow. That's true love.

Timothy   True love, I don't know about that . . .

Lily (*re: picture*)   Look at you. I've never known true love.

Timothy   I don't know if you would call it true love.

Lily   I've only known passion.

Pause. **Timothy** *starts to walk, off.*

Lily   No, look how much you loved each other, look at this.

He turns. She holds up the album, shows him a picture.

Timothy   Yeah . . . But you wouldn't say we got along usually.

She keeps looking through the album.

There was a time we partied a lot and that wasn't good. There's nothing you can do when certain things happen. You can wait for them to be over. Looking back. You wouldn't say we had a good marriage. Things just happen. But you look back. It's strange. I do wonder why God let me live. I did lots of things there was no need to do. We wasted a lot of years. I drove trucks. I was gone a lot . . .

Lily   How'd it happen? Shed never said.

Pause.

Timothy   We went out to dinner. I was driving back. We had wine. I just drove wrong.

Pause.

I was trying to pass a car that was going so slow. I was tired. – I wasn't working, we were talking about that. I was telling her we had to figure something out. We had debt. I pay child support. Shed's been paying the rent. She was just working part-time and I wasn't, I wasn't working, we were trying to figure something out. It was an old lady – she was driving so slow. I misjudged it. I drove my whole life. You get cocky . . .

Pause. **Lily** *holds open the album, angles it towards* **Timothy**. *He does not look at the pictures.*

Timothy   There's probably nothing in my future. Stupid leg.

Lily   But you have your leg now.

Timothy   You can tell. I still limp. The color is wrong.

Lily   I've never had true love. At least you've had that.

Timothy   I don't know . . .

Lily   It was true love.

Pause. **Timothy** *moves to the album, focuses on one photo, just stares at it.*

Timothy   True love . . .

Door opens. **Shed** *enters, wearing a face mask.* **Timothy** *looks up.*

Timothy   Home from work!

Lily   Hey!

Shed *takes off his face mask.* **Timothy** *walks, off.*

Lily   Smell getting to you?

Shed *crosses to the couch, puts down his backpack.*

Shed   Bad tonight.

Lily   Been a while.

Shed   What's up.

Lily   You doing good?

Shed *shrugs. Pause.*

Lily   You got a job!

Shed *nods.*

Lily   I'm – going home, I'm going back, so . . . I'm leaving tomorrow . . . Dave says hi.

Shed   Dave says hi.

Lily   He says you don't answer the phone anymore.

Shed   Got rid of it.

Pause.

Lily   He says he came here, he says you don't answer the door either.

Shed   Don't answer the door, no.

Lily   You sent him his money in the mail?

Shed   Yup.

Pause.

Lily   You didn't miss much. Dave's back with Maryanne. He stays in his room, doesn't leave the apartment, he bought all these gas masks and night-vision goggles. Tell me about your job, it sounds brilliant.

Shed   It's good.

Lily   It's at the hotel?

Shed   Yeah.

Lily   How'd you get it?

Shed   Just went there. Looked right, I guess. Knew how to act.

Lily   When did you start?

Shed   End of August.

Lily   What's it like, you like it?

Shed   Beautiful. It's this guy, Ian Schrager. He has a
shitload of hotels. This one, you go in there, it's like the
world don't exist. It's like, you got a escalator. Lime-green
light. You go up, it's all dark, there's big plants everywhere,
like growing out the walls. Huge chandeliers, like. It's so
cool, it's got, like, special effects – like those 3D things,
holograms and shit. Everybody wear a uniform, like.
Beautiful women waitresses. Outdoor courtyard, trees, big
chairs. Matt Damon's having his birthday party there in a
couple weeks, they got famous people all the time in there,
go there.

Lily   Wow. I love Matt Damon.

Pause.

Yeah. I got you – I wanted to give you something to remind
you of me.

*She reaches into her pocket and pulls out a photo-booth photograph. She
hands it to him.*

Three pictures of me. The first one is the crazy me, see. The
second one is the sad me. The third one is the real me, no
expression.

Shed *looks at the photograph.*

Lily   I was thinking of lifting my top for the last one, but,
you know, it was in the arcade, I felt weird.

Shed   Thanks.

Pause.

Lily   Plus, you don't know where those pictures end up, if
they stay in the computer or whatever. Don't want my tits
all over the place, even if I do have nice tits. – I think I
might miss you the most, you know.

Shed   Yeah?

Pause.

Lily   Anyway. – You gotta give me something before I go.

Shed What?

Lily Something to remember you by. I gave you my picture now you gotta give me something.

Pause. **Shed** *looks around.*

Shed Don't know what I got.

Pause. **Shed** *looks at her. She moves to him and hugs him hard. Pause. She reaches down to his crotch.*

Lily I knew it!

She laughs. Pause. She moves her hand on his crotch. **Shed** *removes her shirt. They look at each other a beat, then embrace.*

Scene Twelve

A bar. Loud music. **Stephen** *stands alone.* **Leo** *approaches. Pause.*

Leo YOU LOOK FAMILIAR.

Stephen I DO?

Leo HAVEN'T WE MET?

Stephen I DON'T THINK SO.

Leo I DON'T KNOW WHY I THINK SO. ARE YOU HERE ALONE?

Stephen YEAH.

Leo WHY DO I THINK I KNOW YOU? DO YOU COME HERE A LOT?

Stephen NO.

Leo WHY NOT?

Stephen WHEN I HAD A BOYFRIEND, I DIDN'T GO OUT.

Leo WHEN DID YOU BREAK UP?

Stephen   A WHILE AGO.

Leo   WHAT HAPPENED?

Stephen   I DON'T KNOW. HE BROKE UP WITH
ME.

Leo   WHY?

Stephen   WHY DO PEOPLE BREAK UP WITH
PEOPLE?

Leo   YOU MISS HIM?

Stephen *doesn't answer, swigs on his beer.*

Leo   YOU DON'T WANT TO TALK ABOUT IT?

Stephen   NOT PARTICULARLY.

Pause.

Leo   WHERE DO YOU LIVE?

Stephen   NEAR HERE.

Pause.

Leo   DO YOU WANT TO GO THERE?

Scene Thirteen

Stephen's *bedroom.* **Stephen** *and* **Leo** *enter.*

Leo   I'm serious, it makes perfect sense. This was
Giuliani's greatest fantasy and his greatest fear. He's always
had a fascist impulse, which this fits perfectly. But,
remember last summer, he had prostate cancer, and there
was all that media coverage about how he might be
impotent. Months later the two tallest most phallic buildings
in New York City go down. What was happening in his
body, happening in his city.

Stephen   Huh. That's really interesting.

Leo *takes out cocaine, does a bump.* **Leo** *gives* **Stephen** *cocaine.* **Stephen** *sniffs cocaine.*

Leo   What's funniest is he's just *like* the Taliban – obsessed with forcing his rules, his ideology, violently upon the people: close down the clubs where gays congregate, shut down the strip clubs where women reveal their bodies, cancel funding for art museums who show art that subverts his religious beliefs: he probably *deeply* identifies with the Taliban.

Stephen   Right . . .

Leo   – Is this the window?

Stephen   That's the window.

Leo *looks out the window. Long pause. The sound of a fighter jet passing.*

Leo   The F-14s are flying low tonight.

He turns to **Stephen**.

Leo (*brightly*)   So. What are we going to do now that we've moved out of a public space and into a private one?

Stephen (*smiling*)   Have sex.

Leo *laughs. He looks around and finds a photograph.*

Leo   Is this your boyfriend?

Stephen   Ex. Yeah.

Leo   What was his name?

Stephen   Why do you want to know?

Leo   I dunno.

Stephen   Tyler. I'm gonna brush my teeth.

Leo   Okay.

Stephen *exits, off.* **Leo** *stares at the photograph. Then he puts it down and takes off his shoes.* **Stephen** *enters.*

Stephen   Hey.

Leo   Hey. Have you heard from him since the eleventh?

Stephen   Who?

Leo   Tyler.

Stephen   No . . .

Leo   No?

Stephen   Nope.

Leo   I don't believe in love.

Stephen   You don't?

Leo   No, I think it's a vague word that is applied indiscriminately.

Stephen (*laughs*)   Oh.

Leo   To me, a more interesting question is what people are doing to each other in each other's company under the guise of 'love'.

Stephen   What do you mean?

Leo   Like – what is love? What *is* it? I mean, you can say, okay – okay, this person fucks me, he calls me, he eats meals with me, he tells me about his day, I am in his thoughts and fantasies, I do things and he has feelings about them – you can make a list of facts. But what makes those facts love? What? And – I couldn't figure it out. So I decided there was no such thing. And that I was fine with that.

Stephen   Uh-huh.

Leo *begins removing his clothes.*

Leo   The idea of love is so heteronormative, and it's perfect for capitalism: it prevents people from thinking about real problems in their lives, it makes them think, when they feel bad, that something is wrong with them and not the world, it makes people form families and buy things for those families . . . (*He's in his boxers.*) You're so adorable.

Stephen   You too.

Stephen *turns out the light. We can barely see them. They undress.*

Leo   Put on some music.

He gets in bed. **Stephen** *puts music on – R & B. He goes into bed.* **Leo** *begins to fellate* **Stephen***, then kisses him.* **Leo** *gets on top of* **Stephen** *and begins moving.*

Leo   Mmm.

Stephen   That feels good.

Leo   You like that?

Stephen   Yeah.

Leo *continues.* **Stephen** *turns him over and gets on top of him and kisses him.*

Leo   You can kiss.

Stephen (*laughs*)   I can?

Leo   Mm-hmm.

They kiss. **Leo** *wraps his legs around* **Stephen***. Then* **Leo** *takes his own hands and puts them behind his head. He takes* **Stephen***'s right hand and clasps it to his two hands, as if to restrain them.*

Leo   Harder.

Stephen *thrusts against* **Leo** *harder. Then* **Leo** *eases* **Stephen** *off him.* **Leo** *gets on his hands and knees.*

Leo (*sweetly*)   Rub against me like you're fucking me.

Stephen *does.*

Leo   That's good. Mm.

He masturbates himself as **Stephen** *rubs against him from behind.*

Leo   Mmmm.

Stephen   Uh. Uh. Uhmm.

Stephen *moves more roughly.* **Leo** *takes* **Stephen**'*s hand from his breast, puts it on top of his head.*

Leo   Pull on my hair a little.

Stephen *does. He arches his neck, kisses* **Leo**.

Leo   Mmmm.

Stephen   Uhhhh. Uhhhhh.

Leo   Mm. You're fine, right?

Stephen   What?

Leo   I'm fine – we're both fine – you don't have – you don't have / HIV.

Stephen   No.

Leo   *More.* Oh God.

Stephen *continues, getting rougher.*

Stephen   You like that?

Leo   *Yes.*

Stephen   Yeah? You like that?

Leo   – Fuck me.

Stephen   Yeah, you want me to fuck you?

Leo   Yes please.

Stephen   Yeah?

Leo   I like it.

Stephen   I like it too. Uh. Uh.

Leo   Go inside me.

Stephen   Yeah?

Leo   You can go inside me.

Stephen (*stopping for a moment*)   Wait – go? – literally?

Leo   Please fuck me.

Stephen   I / don't –

Leo   Please.

Pause. Then **Stephen** *enters him, somewhat awkwardly.* **Leo** *grimaces a little.* **Stephen** *fucks him, slow at first, then faster.*

Leo   Oh my *God* . . . Oh *God* . . . Oh *God* . . .

Stephen   Uhhhhh. Uhhhh, uhhh uhhh –

Leo   Mmmm mm mmmm –

Stephen   Uhh / uhh uhh –

Leo   Mmm mmm mmm mmm / mmm mmm mmm –

Stephen   Uhhhm uuhmm uhuuhmm –

Stephen *stops suddenly.*

Leo   What? Did you come?

Pause. **Stephen** *releases, lies back on the bed.*

Stephen   No . . .

Leo   Why did you stop?

Stephen   I'm sorry.

Pause. **Leo** *grabs* **Stephen**'s *penis and begins to masturbate him.*

Stephen   I'm sorry, I have to stop.

Pause. **Leo** *lies back, masturbates himself. Sound of a fighter jet cutting across the sky. Finally* **Leo** *orgasms.*

Leo   Uhhhhh –

Pause.

Stephen   Let me get you a towel.

He gets **Leo** *a towel and gives it to him.* **Leo** *cleans himself.*
Stephen *turns off music and dresses.* **Leo** *puts the towel on the floor
and dresses. As they do this:*

Stephen   That was interesting, the comparisons you were
making before with the Taliban and Giuliani.

Leo   Uh-huh?

Stephen   I've been reading about Afghanistan – the chaos
of the region. So many tribes – so many different groups –
disconnected, historically, from their / central government.

Leo   Right.

Stephen   Disconnected from their leaders – and
disconnected from each other – all these various groups
occupying the same space without being able to / find a
common –

Leo   Uh-huh.

Stephen   Just – how fractured and isolated they are – like
New York, too, in some ways . . .

Pause. **Leo** *and* **Stephen** *are dressed.* **Leo** *looks at* **Stephen**.

Leo   Nice to meet you.

Stephen   You're gonna go?

Leo *smiles.*

Stephen   ' Are you sure? I could make some tea . . .

Leo   I'm fine. Bye.

Leo *goes, off.* **Stephen** *sits down on his bed. He looks out the
window. Lights rise on* **Timothy**'s *apartment.* **Lily** *is finishing
dressing.* **Shed** *has his boxers on. Pause.*

Lily   – Say a prayer the plane doesn't fly into the Empire
State Building.

Shed   Ha. I will.

Lily   Yeah. So . . . (*Laughs.*) Nice knowing you.

Shed   You too.

Lily   Congrats again on your job, that's really great.

Shed   Yeah . . .

Lily   Yeah . . . we're friends, yeah?

Shed   What you mean?

Lily   We're buddies. We're pals.

Pause.

Shed   Yeah . . .

Lily   Yeah. Anyway . . .

She starts to go.

Shed   Hold on.

She stops.

– It's bad out there – take this.

He hands her his face mask.

Lily   Oh.

She looks at it a beat.

Shed   Here, I do it.

He stands behind her, puts it over her mouth and nose. She stands, still for a moment, then begins to cry.

What's wrong, now?

Lily   Dunno . . .

Shed   It's okay . . .

Lily   Yeah . . . Okay. Bye.

She goes, off. **Shed** *puts on his pants. Turns on video game, sits down.* **Timothy** *enters.*

Timothy   Lily go?

Shed   Yeah.

Pause. **Shed** *plays video game.*

Timothy   Working late tonight?

Shed   Walked home.

Timothy   Oh, you walked home?

Shed   I got laid off.

Timothy   – What?

Shed (*still playing game*)   Nobody in the hotel. Nobody there, tourists not coming, so, they letting the most recent people go.

Timothy   Oh, Christ. You got fired? No!

Shed   And it's like – it's like, I don't understand – what's – wrong with – me –

Shed *starts to cry, puts down video-game controller.*

Timothy   Oh God.

Shed   It's like – I know what not to do, in my life, but I don't – know – what – *to* do, you know?

Timothy   No – that's not – people get / fired.

Shed (*fighting tears with anger*)   I don't know what to DO.

Timothy   You be okay, you'll figure it out.

Shed   Figure out what? What?

Pause.

What are we gonna figure out?

Pause.

What are we gonna do?

Pause.

Timothy   You can't blame yourself. It's just how things –
it's not your fault – it's just the world . . .

Shed *looks at* **Timothy**. *Pause. He opens his backpack, takes out a
carton of cigarettes.*

Shed   Fucking, you believe people pay ten dollars a pack?
In the hotel, if you go on the street, five dollars, ten dollars
inside. They fired me, I took some.

Timothy *smiles.*

Timothy   Thank you.

Shed   Not a problem.

Pause.

Timothy   Maybe . . . I can get a job when I'm done with
rehab. I don't – they say I can't drive a truck, but. It might –
maybe I can drive a van. I might, they / don't know.

Shed   All right.

Timothy   Something, there'll be something – we – we'll
be able to –

Shed   All right, I hear you. Just go – go to sleep.

Pause. **Timothy** *walks, off.* **Shed** *reaches for his backpack, looks
in, takes out two cartons of cigarettes. Puts them on the coffee table.
Goes to stereo. Turns on hip hop. Picks up game controller again,
begins playing. Pause.* **Shed** *pauses the game. He takes one carton
from the table. He exits the apartment, goes to* **Stephen***'s door,
knocks.* **Stephen** *hears. He exits his bedroom and goes to the door.*

Stephen   Hello?

Shed's voice   Hey, it's your neighbor.

Stephen   Yes?

Shed's voice   Got – something for you, wanna open up.

Stephen   What?

Shed's voice   I got something for you.

Pause. **Stephen** *opens the door.*

Stephen   Hey, what's up.

Shed *holds out the carton.*

Shed   Hey – just – got these for you, you know . . .

Stephen   Oh. – Thank you . . .

He takes the cigarettes. Pause.

You guys – you guys okay?

Shed   Yeah, we fine.

Stephen   Your – dad's okay?

Shed   My dad. Oh. That's not my dad. That's my uncle. But yeah, he's okay.

Stephen   Oh – good.

Shed   He got his leg finally. They finally gave him his leg, so.

Stephen   That's great.

Shed   That's my uncle. He lived there, I lived there with him and my aunt, but she died in the car accident, where he lost his leg. So it's good he got his leg, so.

Stephen   Oh – oh God.

Pause.

Shed   You see it happen?

Stephen   I – I saw it from my bedroom window. I saw the whole thing.

Shed   Yeah. I went up on the roof . . . saw that . . .

Stephen   Terrible.

Shed   Yeah.

Pause.

Anyway. That's it.

Stephen   Thank you.

Shed   You welcome.

Shed *goes.* **Stephen** *shuts the door.*

Scene Fourteen

Slide reads: October 9, 2001.

The bar. **Patricia** *stands behind the bar. It's empty.* **Stephen** *sits with a soda. An American flag draped, behind the bar.*

Patricia   And then he says, 'So I was thinking you and I would have an affair.'

Stephen   Oh God.

Patricia   Sixty-two years old, this man. I'm telling you – visual artists.

Stephen   Painters are so weird . . .

Patricia   What's wrong with them?

Stephen   Aren't they stuck at the anal stage? Isn't paint – isn't it something to do with the child playing with feces? I think I read that in Freud.

Young Businessman 1 *enters, sits at the end of the bar.*

Patricia   Hey there, Howard.

Howard (Young Businessman 1)   Hey, Patricia.

Howard *looks up at the television.*

Stephen (*quietly*)   How's he doing?

Patricia   I haven't seen him in a week.

She goes over to him.

You want a Stella?

Howard   Thank you.

She gets him a beer.

How's business?

Patricia   It's picking up. People still aren't eating out, but they're drinking.

Howard   That's good. I need this beer, Jesus.

Patricia   Yeah? What's going on, is there any news about Ron? Have they found his / body yet?

Howard   They're not gonna find him, it's all just ash, they should give / up.

The bar phone rings. Pause. **Howard** *motions for her to answer.*

Patricia (*picks up*)   Hello?

Howard *turns to* **Stephen**.

Howard   It's weird. I was at the subway, just now . . . The train was late, like five minutes. That happens all the time. But I started getting pissed off. And more and more people started coming down, into the station. And the train kept not coming. Kept looking down the tunnel. Nothing. No announcement. Must have been two, maybe three hundred people on the platform. And I thought – I started getting, like, claustrophobic.

Patricia *hangs up the phone, listens.*

Howard   And I knew – I knew the train would come. Rationally – I knew – trains are late all the time. But I had this feeling – like something was gonna happen. Even though I knew, I knew the train would come, nothing was wrong, there was just some delay. But it was like – like if I didn't get out of there, something bad was gonna happen. And I left – left the station, walked here.

Stephen   Wow.

Howard   I'm a rational guy. I knew the train was coming but – blah blah blah.

Howard *sips beer. Pause.*

Patricia   Market's doing better.

Howard   Market's fine. – It just doesn't make sense . . . how something that was there goes away . . .

Howard *looks up at the stock ticker on the TV.* **Patricia** *moves to* **Stephen**.

Patricia   What are you doing tonight?

Stephen   I was actually thinking of taking a walk down there. Be a witness. Say that I saw it. I was there. This is what it was like.

On the TV, footage of George Bush, stock ticker running below.

Howard   That's right. Bomb the shit out of them. Go over there and bomb them to the fucking Dark Ages. (*Chanting.*) U-S-A! U-S-A! U-S-A! (*Laughing.*) Come on, Patricia. Show a little patriotism.

Patricia   That's okay, you got enough for both of us.

Howard (*smiling.*)   Yeah, I do, don't I?

He sips his beer. **Patricia** *turns to* **Stephen**. *She smiles at him.*

Stephen   You're so good with these guys, you know that.

Patricia   What else are you gonna be?

Howard   U-S-A! U-S-A!

He raises his beer.

A toast, what do you say?

Beat. **Stephen** *smiles, raises his soda.* **Patricia** *raises a bottle of water.*

Howard   To the USA!

Stephen   – To where we live.

Patricia   Cheers.

They toast. **Howard** *turns back to TV.* **Patricia** *starts wiping down the bar.* **Stephen** *watches her.*

Dying City

Dying City was first performed at the Royal Court Jerwood Theatre Upstairs, London, on 12 May 2006. The cast was as follows:

Kelly   Sian Brooke
Peter/Craig Andrew Scott

Director James Macdonald
Lighting and Set Designer Peter Mumford
Sound Designer Ian Dickinson

Characters

Kelly, *late twenties*
Peter, *late twenties*
Craig, *late twenties*

Craig *and* **Peter** *are identical twins and played by the same actor.*

The play takes place in January 2004 and July 2005.

Note

No interval; blackouts should be avoided; sound between scenes should not be overdesigned.

The play takes place in Kelly's apartment. A combined kitchen and living room; doors lead to a bathroom and bedroom off. I imagined a design that lives in naturalism but suggests something beyond it. I've kept stage directions to a minimum, omitting obvious actions in an attempt to avoid clutter.

Scene One

Night. **Kelly** *sorts through books. A cardboard box sits next to the couch. TV plays* Law and Order. *A bedsheet and pillow are scrunched up in the corner of the couch. The buzzer buzzes.*

Kelly   Hello?

Peter's voice   Hi – it's Peter!

Pause.

Kelly   Hi!

Peter's voice   I tried calling . . .

Pause.

Kelly   Come up!

Pause. She throws the bedsheet over the box. **Peter** *knocks.*

Hi! Peter . . .

Peter   Hi, Kelly – sorry!

Kelly   Come in.

Peter   You're unlisted now!

Kelly   I am . . .

Peter   I tried calling your landline, and then I tried your cell – I was wondering, I thought maybe it was a *work* thing, maybe one of your clients got your numbers or something and you / had to change –

Kelly   It's – yeah, it's – I've been meaning to call you and – it's – I just haven't. I've been so / busy –

Peter   Oh, no, of course –

Kelly   I wanted to make sure I had the, that I had enough – energy, mental space, before I called . . .

Peter   Did you, I wasn't – did you get my letter?

Kelly   I did.

Peter   I was wondering, I wasn't sure if I had the right
address –

Kelly   I did. Yeah, and I just – I've been *meaning* to call –

Peter   No – of *course*.

Kelly   So . . .

Pause.

Well – sit down, please! I'll make some tea.

Peter   Oh, tea would be lovely.

Kelly   Were you – in the neighborhood or – you're in
town visiting . . . ?

Peter   – I know, barging in like this, I have to apologize.

Kelly   Well – I don't have a phone.

Peter (*laughs*)   Right. No, I didn't plan on – tonight – it's
actually a bit of a *drama* actually.

Kelly   Oh?

Pause.

Peter   I'm sorry, is everything – did I, is it a bad – a bad /
time or –

Kelly   No. No.

Peter   I just . . .

Pause.

Kelly   You know, honestly – when they come to tell you –

Pause.

When they came to tell me about Craig, they just showed
up – they just / show up, no warning, they don't call or –

Peter   Oh God. Oh Kelly, I'm so sorry. I'm so *stupid*.

Kelly   So I was just – a memory . . .

Peter   Of *course.*

Kelly   . . . of the buzzer – I'm fine.

Peter   God, I'm a total idiot.

Kelly   I'm fine.

Peter   And it's just about a year, right?

Kelly   Last week. Yeah.

Peter   Last *week.* Huh. I've been – the date was sort of floating around in my head but I've been kind of distracted because of these other . . . I've been thinking a lot about the *funeral,* actually.

Kelly   Uh-huh?

Peter   Just how weird it was.

Kelly   Yeah.

Peter   No one really talking.

Kelly   Mm. No one knew what to *say.*

Peter   About?

Kelly   Just – you know, the shock. Everyone was in shock.

Peter   Okay. I thought you meant – knew what to say, like, weren't sure what to say because it seemed like maybe what happened wasn't what the military was saying.

Kelly   Oh.

Peter   Did you feel that at all? I don't know, maybe I'm crazy, but I felt that underneath a little, that people kind of thought it wasn't an accident maybe, and that's why everyone was so quiet.

Kelly   Well. The way it was told to us – so many of his men saw it happen . . .

Peter   Yeah – I guess I thought maybe, because everyone there knew that Dad taught us, from the time we were little, how to shoot, how to handle weapons, that maybe some people didn't believe the story.

Kelly   Right. Well, the investigation was still going on at that point, it wasn't official, so some people might have felt that.

Peter   Yeah. And maybe it's a gun culture thing, we grew up around guns, you didn't, so it's something I would feel more than you . . . *Target* practice, I just . . . Craig would always write about how careful he was with his weapon – I still can't picture it.

Kelly   It's a hard thing to picture.

Pause.

Peter   Another thing that sucked was I could only be there for one *day*, remember? I had to fly back and do those stupid reshoots on my movie. The whole thing was so, it's like this *blur* – dealing with Mom, two years after Dad – and, like, the whole *gay* thing, do these people know, or not, and no one *talking* to me – except you.

Kelly   – How is your mom?

Peter   Oh, the same. I don't know what it will take to pierce that woman's heart, but . . .

Pause.

Kelly   Well – I'm glad you're here. However. It's great to see you.

Peter   A bit weird maybe?

Kelly   Weird – a little. How you look.

Peter   Yeah, I always think of that . . . A relief, though, too.

Kelly   Uh-huh . . . ?

Peter   That's how *I* feel. Even though it's hard. To finally see you again. – Not since the funeral, God! Even *spoken*!

Kelly   *Time.* I can't believe so much time has passed –

Peter   It feels like yesterday, right? – I wonder if the
anniversary – because I wasn't aware of the exact date – if
that had anything to do with what happened tonight.

Kelly   – What happened?

Peter   I . . . I did something sort of shocking.

Pause.

I'm sorry.

Kelly   What?

Peter   I know I've already said this, but I can't believe I
just showed up like this. Because – we talked, at the funeral,
about what it was *like* for you when they just showed up and
buzzed – and here I go do the exact same thing!

Kelly   You didn't have my number, what other way could
you have gotten in / touch?

Peter   I know, but still . . .

Kelly   It's fine. Really. Forget about it.

Pause. **Peter** *smiles.*

Peter   Oh, all right, if you *insist* . . .

Kelly *smiles.*

Peter   Was it – is everything okay, I mean . . . ?

Kelly   With . . . ?

Peter   Did you have to change your numbers because of a
client, did something happen?

Kelly   – Oh.

Peter   I always worried something *stalkery* would happen
to you, you're so beautiful.

Kelly   – Oh!

Peter I'm serious! Therapy, you know, two people alone in a room, it's very sexy! – Not that I've ever *done* it. In my fantasies – 'the handsome Doctor . . .'

Kelly – You take sugar, right? I only have whole milk –

Peter Plain is fine.

Kelly Plain?

Peter Yes – I'm playing this *assassin* in this movie I have coming up, I'm supposed to be getting in shape – I have this *trainer* . . .

Kelly He's tough?

Peter *She* – the guy-trainers I've had, it's weird, I think they've all been jealous of me – my manager thinks it's because I'm so handsome. – But yes, she is tough.

Kelly It's funny, you know, you say what you imagine therapy is like – when I first started I thought I'd get to hear people talk about sex, their sex lives? But it's food. People want to talk about eating – their *body* image, their *eating* habits –

Peter That's so pathetic.

Kelly It's really what people are obsessed with.

Peter Yeah, because nobody fucks anymore, they just eat like pigs instead!

Pause.

Kelly I don't know about that. Viagra's still pretty popular . . .

Peter That's true, I guess . . . Right! *There's* your problem – the people who would have gone to therapy and talked about sex are all just popping Viagra instead!

Kelly Huh . . .

Peter – Oh, but, what about fucked-her-so-hard-she? *He* wanted to talk about sex.

A moment. Then:

Kelly   – What?

Peter   It just came into my head, your client – we talked about him on Craig's last night. – That was what we called him, right? Fucked-her-so- / hard-she?

Kelly   – Wow, you remember that?

Peter   We talked about him half the night, how could I forget?! Coming up with our little theories about him – *Tim* thought he should go on Prozac, of course.

Kelly   – How *is* Tim? Nice to hear his name . . .

Peter   Tim's well, he's well. Just went back to Los Angeles, yesterday actually – school's starting in a month, month and a half, so . . .

Kelly   You guys were here . . . ?

Peter   He just came to visit – I've been here – I'm doing a play . . . ?

Kelly   – *That's* right.

Peter   *Long Day's Journey into Night* –

Kelly   Of course – in the letter you – yes.

Peter   So . . . he was out for the opening in April, then came back after school got out . . . I've been here since *February*, God.

Kelly   – I remember now. So you've been here a while!

Peter   Yeah, it has been . . .

Kelly   And Tim went back to get ready for school?

Peter   Another year of figuring out how to get inner-city eighth-graders interested in *Romeo and Juliet*. Hopeless . . .

Kelly   – You should go to his class, do a dramatic reading.

Peter   I suggested that! But he has this idea that it would be 'disruptive'. Since I'm 'famous'.

Kelly   I can see that.

Peter   Oh, please, my movie *tanked*. Did you see it?

Kelly   You know – I usually wait for the / DVD –

Peter   Oh God, it was *so* stinky – oh!

Kelly   Really? I've always been curious about that process – because I remember you said it was a good script. So how does it become a bad / movie?

Peter   Right – I was just about to start shooting, on Craig's last night, we talked about it . . . Why are we – who cares about my career, how boring!

Kelly   It's not boring to *me* –

Peter   To me it's like the least interesting – I guess we all get bored talking about work. Of course *I* want to know about fucked-her-so-hard-she, you probably find talking about *that* boring.

Kelly   – I can't believe you remember that. You have such / a good –

Peter   We had such an interesting debate on how you should handle him! *I* thought he was lying just to sound interesting, Tim thought he was self-medicating – Craig didn't think he was *lying*, just that he wanted to torture you – and didn't actually want to get better.

Kelly   Craig the expert –

Peter   Fucked-her-so-hard-she . . . What happened with him, how did things turn / out?

Kelly   – I have to say, I hated that nickname Craig gave him. It was so crass.

Peter   But – wasn't that how the guy himself – didn't he, say, like –

Kelly   It was how he would phrase his conquests –

Peter   Which is all he ever would talk about, right? And he would always use the same phrase – 'I fucked her so hard she came six times.'

Kelly   Yes –

Peter   'I fucked her so hard she started crying' – 'I fucked her so hard she – woke up my ninety-year-old hearing-impaired neighbor' –

Kelly   Well – he didn't go *that* far. – You know, it slipped my mind a second ago – but I have to say – I read a number of just incredible reviews for the play. You opened in April you said?

Peter *makes 'masturbation' motion.*

Kelly   What?

Peter   – It's a terrible production.

Kelly   No.

Peter *nods.*

Kelly   I had made a plan to come and just never got around / to it –

Peter   You're not missing anything.

Kelly   What's – wrong with it?

Peter   It's not true.

Pause.

Kelly   I'm sorry to hear that.

Peter   Yeah. 'Oh well!' (*Smiles.*) The 'drama' is actually – I'm still kind of in shock, I think – but the drama is that I walked offstage tonight – in the middle of the show.

Pause.

Kelly   – Oh.

Peter   Yeah.

Kelly   I was going to – because I remember it being a pretty long / play –

Peter   Yeah.

Pause.

Kelly   – Is your tea okay . . . ?

Peter   No, it's because there isn't any sugar. I don't want to drink it.

Kelly   Oh – would you like / some –

Peter   No – I can't.

Pause.

Yeah. Right before the intermission – my dad is calling me from offstage, 'Come on, Edmund!' I make my exit and there he is – Tyrone, John Conrad – you know him, right? Very big / man –

Kelly   Mm-hmm –

Peter   So he sort of beckons me over, like, with this look on his face like he has a joke to tell me, or some little piece of gossip. So I go over, I lean into him, he grabs my shoulder and whispers into my ear, 'I have a piece of advice for you.' He says, 'You're never –'

Pause.

He says, 'You're never going to be a good actor till you stop sucking cock.'

Kelly   – Oh.

Peter   Applause, act's over, I'm standing there *stunned*, he's looking at me and smiling this, this *smile*, and then he takes me, it's sort of like he's shoving me aside, but, like, *really* hard –

Kelly   Oh, Peter.

Peter   – I thought about going to the stage manager, telling her what happened, but John is the star, and no one else *saw*, so he can just *lie* and – you know, in rehearsals, with John, and Scott, the director – I talked about *Dad* dying of leukemia, I talked about *Craig* dying in Iraq, I – and so I'm in my dressing room at this point, all alone, imagining having to go back out there with this man and pour my heart out to him and – I looked in the mirror and I just grabbed my stuff and left.

Pause.

Kelly   You did the right thing.

Peter   I didn't, though – I should have gone to the stage manager. I fucked up the whole second half of the / show.

Kelly   You can do all the formal stuff tomorrow – I'm sure you have an understudy.

Peter   *Drew.* He like does coke and gets escorts, I don't even think he knows the lines.

Kelly   Well. You'll straighten it out tomorrow.

Pause.

Peter   Then the *other* thing is – I broke up with Tim last night.

Kelly   You broke up with / Tim?

Peter*'s mobile rings, he checks it.*

Peter   I should . . .

Kelly *nods.* **Peter** *gestures towards the bedroom.* **Kelly** *nods again.* **Peter** *answers the phone as he moves into the bedroom, off . . .*

Scene Two

Night. **Kelly** *cleans up.* **Craig** *comes out of the bedroom, helps.*

Craig   He's wasted.

Kelly   He's wasted? He didn't drink that much.

Craig   He's passed out . . .

Kelly   He just had two cups of coffee!

Craig   Yeah, with enough sugar to light up a room full of third-graders.

Kelly   Well, he *can't* be passed out for long.

Craig   It's ridiculous at his age. Ever since he was little – used to pour sugar on top of his Frosted Flakes, drove Dad crazy –

Kelly   *Ohhh.*

Craig   What?

Kelly   I bet he took a Xanax.

Craig   A Xanax?

Kelly   You were in the bathroom. Tim had Xanax for the plane, he hates flying.

Craig   What happened when I was in the bathroom?

Kelly   We were talking about Black Hawks –

Craig   Yeah –

Kelly   You got up to pee, and Tim said he couldn't imagine doing what you did because he couldn't even fly on a *commercial* plane without taking a Xanax. Then he took a bottle out of his pocket and shook it for effect.

Craig   'Shook it for effect'?

Kelly   It was cute.

Craig   So Peter took one?

Kelly   Not at the table – I'm just guessing – at some point.

Craig   But they're not prescribed to him.

Pause.

Kelly *Well . . .*

Craig That's a powerful drug! He's not a doctor. I bet this shit flows in Hollywood / like fucking –

Kelly One Xanax, I mean –

Craig Yeah, one Xanax and he's so fucked up he can't even talk, he's in there *drooling.*

Pause.

Kelly So maybe he took two.

Craig Why are you being flip? You're against these drugs.

Kelly In my *work* – when people medicate so they don't have to look at their problems – not as a once-in-a-while / thing.

Craig I'm going to Fort Benning in the morning and now I can't even say goodbye to him!

Pause.

Kelly I'm sorry. How are you feeling?

Craig A little agitated. I mean I'm *fine* . . . How are you?

Kelly All things considered . . .

Craig Yeah?

Pause.

I guess it was a nice night.

Kelly It was.

Craig He was nervous, but – I thought he'd be much worse.

Kelly Peter or Tim?

Craig Peter.

Kelly You really do overestimate his attachment to you.

Craig   I know you think that –

Kelly   I think you need to be on the outside to see it. He's
not seven anymore, copying the way you walk and talk.
Look at when we were talking about Iraq – we really got
into it!

Craig (*a realization*)   I think *I* was more nervous than I
expected.

Kelly   Really? You didn't seem nervous to me.

Craig   No?

Kelly   At most I would say – you were a little more
'animated' than usual.

Craig   I thought it got most intense when we were talking
about his career. That's where I felt maybe I went too far.

Kelly   – It's amazing, isn't it? Peter's gonna be a movie
star! He's gonna be rich!

Craig   That movie sounded so fucking offensive.

Kelly   Yeah, but I agree with Peter, within the confines of
what they / make today –

Craig   That's the thing. You start telling yourself / that –

Kelly   – But think why we don't have any Brandos or
James Deans anymore – they're not, it's all so corporate-
controlled, nobody's writing parts that a Brando or a –
imagine Marlon Brando doing *Titanic*. James Dean in *Lord of
the Rings*, I mean –

Craig   But I'm talking about – yes, all the capitalist,
corporate, I know Peter's not going to be in *Rebel Without a
Cause* his first movie out – but I'm talking about Peter saying
he thought the movie was *good*. *That's* what makes / me –

Kelly   Within the *confines* of what they produce today.

Craig   But that's exactly what – why can't he just say, 'It's
a bad movie, it's a piece of shit, but I have to start

somewhere'? What does that mean, 'good within the confines'? You could say that about any movie, basically. Peter's too smart to start thinking that / way –

Kelly   Well, we don't know anything about the movie.

Craig   Yeah, but from what he said – 'special forces' – 'covert operations' – come on. I mean, do the movie, fine, but don't trick yourself about what it is.

Pause.

Kelly   I think it was a good night.

Craig   Yeah . . . Yeah. Why not? Let's call it a good night.

Kelly   It was.

Craig   Just . . . I wanted to say goodbye in a more formal way.

Kelly   – So wake him up.

Craig   Nah, moment's gone.

Pause.

Kelly   – You brought up fucked-her-so-hard-she, that threw me for a loop.

Craig   Oh God – it just came out . . .

Kelly   Out of *nowhere* . . .

Craig   I was thinking out loud. – I was pretty drunk there, till you put the coffee on.

Kelly   Why were you thinking about *him?*

Craig   Just – I don't know, you're seeing him in the morning . . .

Kelly   So?

Craig   Just – crossed my mind.

Pause.

Kelly   I forgot for a second.

Craig   What?

Kelly   Morning . . .

Pause.

Craig   – At least it got Tim talking, finally.

Kelly   What?

Craig   Fucked-her-so-hard-she. Tim thought he was 'clinically depressed'.

Kelly   He was very articulate, I thought.

Craig   No, yeah – I liked him. Did you like him?

Kelly   Oh, definitely! They're great together.

Craig   Yeah . . . A little quiet . . .

Kelly   I'm sure he was *nervous* – meeting his boyfriend's identical *twin* –

Craig   No, I know . . . You didn't think anything was off with him?

Kelly   No, not at all.

Craig   I don't know, I had this little nagging, like – just this feeling that something was off. Like – like I couldn't picture them fucking.

Kelly   Craig!

Craig   Just, the vibe wasn't – whatever, he's better than the Psychopath.

Kelly   Oh, Craig.

Craig   I know you had a soft spot for him –

Kelly   I actually didn't – but Adam was not a psychopath. He had *quirks*, he had *issues* –

Craig   Quirks?

Kelly   Whatever you want to call them. His personality was *affected* by the abuse he suffered. That doesn't make / him a –

Craig   – The abuse he *claimed* to have suffered.

Kelly   Well, we don't know if he did or not.

Craig   Wait – I thought you told Peter it never happened, the abuse.

Kelly   I told Peter it was *possible* it never happened. I / can't –

Craig   That's not what he told me – he told me you told him you thought Adam made it up.

Kelly   Well . . . that's not what I said.

Craig   So you think it's possible that Adam's older brother forced him to give blow jobs to all the boys in the neighborhood, every day after school for two years, when he was six years / old –

Kelly   I think it's unlikely. But what I told Peter is that the memories could be an elaboration of something *less* severe that *did* happen. Or a fantasy that he got mixed up with reality because he was so young at the time / he –

Craig   – Or a lie. Meant to make Peter feel guilty, so he'd never dump Adam.

Kelly   Or that. – The point is, even if it isn't in any way *literally* true, the fact that Adam goes around telling people that this happened means he feels that something traumatic *did* happen to him when he was a boy, and that this 'story' is the only way he has of communicating that trauma. You know, his parents were clearly very / disturbed –

Craig   See – this is what worries me about you. You're the same way with fucked-her-so-hard-she, you're so passive, or finding / ways to –

Kelly   – Can you stop calling him that now?

Craig   – What?

Kelly   It was one thing when it was just between us, but – he's a human being.

Craig   I'm just saying – if you know someone is manipulating you, then you should tell them, Look, I know what you're doing, stop it.

Kelly   Even if he *were* manipulating me – if I said that, he would never come back to therapy!

Craig   So what! At least this way he would know, he would have to walk around knowing that someone knew the truth!

Kelly   The purpose of therapy is to help someone change, not just / face the truth –

Craig   That's what I'm saying – people like that don't want to change, they just want to see what they can get away with –

Kelly   Stop.

Pause.

This always happens when we talk seriously about my work.

Craig   We don't talk seriously about your work.

Kelly   Exactly, / because –

Craig   Okay –

Kelly   – you treat me like I'm this ridiculous person. Which does not make me feel *good*, or *loved*, / or –

Craig   Okay –

Kelly   Every time we talk about therapy or money, you get revved up, you / start getting –

Craig   Money?

Kelly   Yes – like tonight, when Tim started talking about his upbringing, you did the exact same thing you used to do

when Adam would talk about growing up on the Upper
East Side, or going to Horace / Mann –

Craig   Adam – / no –

Kelly   You turned off. You did. I think *that's* what was 'off'
to you about Tim – that he comes from money. It's why you
have problems with my *dad*, it's why *therapy* / bothers you –

Craig   Problems with your dad?

Kelly   When you criticize his lifestyle, his / attitude –

Craig   My problem with your dad is that he didn't love
you. And the thing that was off to me about Tim – was that
they didn't leave together.

Pause.

Kelly   I did think that was weird.

Pause.

Maybe Peter wanted to say goodbye to you alone.

Craig   Then why did he – ? I don't know, something
didn't feel right.

Kelly   I'm sure that's it.

Pause.

Craig   – I also thought it was weird how much his phone
kept ringing. Agents and managers call so late? How many
times do they need to call?

Pause.

Kelly   Speaking of late . . .

Pause.

Craig   Yeah . . .

Pause.

– Okay. Do up the couch, I'll move Peter out / here –

Kelly   – What?

Craig   What?

Kelly   He's *staying*?

Craig   On the couch . . .

Kelly   Craig – I said, if he comes, is this going to turn into an all-night thing? You said / no –

Craig   Kelly, he can't even –

Kelly   You said no. *Craig* –

Craig   Okay –

Pause.

Okay. I'll call him a car.

Pause.

Kelly   Thank you.

Pause. **Craig** *kisses* **Kelly**. *He goes into the bedroom, off.*

Scene Three

Kelly *watches TV.* **Peter** *comes out of the bedroom.*

Peter   You painted!

Kelly   Oh – yeah.

Peter   White!

Kelly   Brighten things up . . .

Peter   It looks good. – I'm interrupting your *Law and Order*.

Kelly   Oh, I can watch it whenever.

Peter   Tivo?

Kelly   Yeah. I programmed it to record *Law and Order* whenever it's on – an endless / stream –

Peter   I see mine rerun all the time, it's so humiliating.

Kelly   You're kidding! Why have I never seen it?

Peter   Skater pothead: 'Wha? Naw, man, I wasn't in the park that night.'

Kelly   Very good!

Peter (*sitting*)   Please – the casting director just wanted to fuck me. I told him I couldn't skate, he said, 'Oh, it's okay, there's not much skating' – they send me the shooting script, of course I'm on a skateboard in *every* scene.

Kelly   I used to not like *Law and Order*, but then it really started to grow on me.

Peter   Oh yeah?

Kelly   I have this theory about / it –

Peter   – When did you start watching all this TV? I don't remember you being a big TV person.

Kelly   Yeah, I never was before.

Peter   Was it after Craig died?

Pause.

Kelly   Maybe – when I couldn't sleep I'd watch TV, I'd / watch –

Peter   I had trouble sleeping –

Kelly   – these shows –

Peter   The worst time for me was actually *months* after – when the official report came out that said it was an accident. After that I just couldn't sleep for some reason.

Kelly   Yeah, the grief comes at different times, it's so unpredictable. – But I came up with this theory – would you like to hear / it?

Peter   – Oh, definitely!

Kelly   Well, I realized that all these shows, all the *Law and Orders* and all the rip-offs, have the same exact structure: someone dies, and a whole team of specialists springs up to figure out how to solve the mystery of the person's death.

Peter   Right?

Kelly   Which I think is a fantasy people have – that they won't be forgotten. That their death won't just be accepted and mourned, but that an entire *community* will come together, all these special people – lawyers and scientists and forensics experts, judges, detectives – who are devoted, who will not stop until the mystery of the death is solved. And therefore symbolically reversed.

Peter   Wow!

Kelly   Only took me six thousand episodes to figure it out.

Peter   Good use of *insomnia* . . . It's weird with me, lately – I've been *sleeping* fine, but then out of nowhere, doing the play, like – like the other night. I had this fantasy, this image almost, of a Black Hawk helicopter crashing through the ceiling of the theater.

Kelly   – While you were onstage?

Peter   At the curtain call – and curtain calls have always been kind of weird for me, I sort of forget who I am – am I me, or am I the character? But lately, it's like – I feel like *Craig* in the curtain call. And I thought – well, it makes sense, that's how I started acting, when I was little, I would pretend that I was him . . . So maybe it's a delayed grief reaction, like?

Kelly   – It may be . . .

Peter   Tim thinks I have post-traumatic stress disorder, keeps bugging me to see his shrink. But I'm like, no – if this is grief, these 'moments' – then I should feel it, right? I don't want to medicate my grief away . . .

Kelly   I'm not a psychiatrist. But I think Tim is right, it
does sound like you should see one.

Peter   Really, you think? Huh. That surprises me. I'll
think about it then . . .

Pause.

I'm sorry – I feel a little silly asking this, but – are you
moving?

Pause.

Kelly   You mean – all the boxes in the / bedroom –

Peter   Not that you wouldn't *tell* me, I / just –

Kelly   I felt like my life had a lot of clutter, that's all.

Peter   Oh, you're putting some things –

Kelly   In storage, clearing space . . .

Peter   . . . painting . . .

Kelly   So . . .

Peter   That's good . . . Hey, you know, I know I
mentioned to you – I don't know if you remember – at the
funeral? I mentioned Craig's emails? From Iraq?

Kelly   Yeah – I remember your mentioning them . . .

Peter   I just realized, I actually have them with me.

Pause.

Kelly   Uh-huh?

Peter   I keep them at the theater, I read them before
shows, and I just grabbed them before I left tonight. Sort of
instinctively . . .

Kelly   Right . . .

Peter   I know – I remember at the funeral your telling me
you and Craig didn't email while he was over there, you just
talked on the phone – something about the distance . . .

Kelly   Email felt weird to me – not intimate.

Peter   Hearing his voice . . .

Kelly   Felt more –

Peter   Right, yeah. But it must – do you ever – now that he's gone, do you ever wish you had anything down on paper, that you could look at, or . . . ?

Kelly   I have other things . . .

Peter   Yeah . . . I guess, too, you were used to distance. I mean – in a way it must seem like he might even be coming back. It's only been a year. He was on active duty four years after you guys finished Harvard, that's such a long time to be away from each other –

Kelly   – Well, but I always knew that that would be over someday. There was a very definite timetable when he would be done. Plus he wasn't fighting. So it was always in the background that he'd be coming back . . . which – isn't the case anymore.

Peter   Right – and you were in grad school, and becoming a therapist, so you were also really busy then, you weren't as settled as you are now . . .

Kelly   Exactly.

Peter   I remember when he got called up again, I thought – because he had done his four years, it's like – I knew you go on Inactive Ready Reserves after, but I just assumed he was done. Starting his life finally writing his dissertation . . . He never complained, though – wouldn't apply for a deferment . . .

Kelly   He felt a lot of loyalty to the army – ROTC paid for school. He couldn't have gone to Harvard without it.

Peter   Well, he also believed in the war. There was that also.

Pause.

I think it's so sad he never finished his PhD. Do you still
have all his Faulkner research?

Kelly   I sent it to your mom.

Peter   Really? She never told me that. Typical. God, for a
woman who wanted both her sons to get out of the
Midwest, she's never stopped resenting us for it. She hasn't
come to see my / *play* –

Kelly   – You think it's that?

Peter   What?

Kelly   You think she resents you because you left your –

Peter   Oh, the social-class thing, definitely, anything to do
with being *educated, cultured*, makes her – I think that was a
big reason she didn't – not that she didn't, doesn't *like*
you, / but –

Kelly   But isn't it also – very generally, that she resents
that her life didn't turn out the way she planned, her
husband dying, her son – I mean, she pushed you and Craig
very hard in school, didn't she? So you could / get out of –

Peter   Oh, and took us to theater, and took us to
museums – but she didn't want us to be cultured so much as
she just wanted us to be able to get away from Dad. When
he got back from Vietnam I think she knew something was –
even from pictures you can tell. But she wasn't going to
leave him, they had us – so she pushed us to excel, go away
to school. . . but once we *did* that – she resented / us.

Kelly   I see. I thought maybe she hadn't told you about
the dissertation because it reminds her of everything – that
hasn't turned out right.

Pause.

Peter   He was such a good writer. These emails – they
could be published. I've thought about maybe trying to
make them into a one-man show. I don't know if I'd play
him. I guess it would make the most sense for me to, but –

feels a little – also – they're so intimate, I don't know if I'd want to share them with people. I haven't shown them to anyone.

Pause.

I'd – love to share them with you if you . . .

Kelly   Oh. That's . . . you know, I just don't think I'm ready.

Pause.

Peter   I understand.

Pause.

You can really see in them how much he learned from you, I think . . . just, his emotions and . . . it's hard because, you didn't know him before you met him obviously, but – the way he blossomed with you – especially after you got married . . . God, it's just about three years, right?

Kelly   Just about. September . . .

Peter   Wow. I remember when you guys finally got engaged, him calling me up to tell me – God, I was so happy. Because I was getting – I was definitely, like, let's hurry it up here!

Kelly   We had always talked about it – he just wanted to wait till he was done with active duty.

Peter   – I also think Dad getting sick definitely – gave him some perspective . . . And 9/11 . . .

Pause.

It's so great that Dad got to see you get married. He looked so happy that day – so cute, so frail and gentle . . . Mom was such a cunt to you at his funeral, do you remember?

Kelly   Of course I remember. I was 'too loud' in the receiving line – I barely said a word.

Pause.

– Was that your director who called before? Is / everything –

Peter   – No, I haven't called him back yet, he just left me a voicemail – I was talking to Tim, actually. He's emailing me all this information on PTSD, so . . .

Pause.

Kelly   I owe you an apology, Peter.

Peter   Uh-huh?

Kelly   I know how important it was to you that I stay in touch. I told you at the funeral that I would – and I didn't.

Peter   Oh, thank you . . . no, definitely, I mean – I'd be lying if I said . . . part of me, you know, definitely did the play hoping being the same city would make us . . . you know, even if it meant going away from Tim, and pissing off my agents . . . make us close again.

Pause.

Kelly   Your letter really – it really did touch me. I should have responded.

Peter   . . . I knew it was a really big thing I was proposing, so I kind of – I expected you to say no, or at least – that you'd need time to think about it . . . But – yeah, you know? I asked you to have a *baby*, I mean, *some* kind of acknowledgment –

Kelly   – I know.

Pause.

Peter   – I hate to do this, but I should call Scott back before it gets too late, is that okay?

Kelly   – Sure.

Peter   Thanks.

He takes out his mobile and goes back into the bedroom.

Scene Four

Craig *comes out of the bedroom.*

Kelly   Hey.

Craig   So, I don't think Peter's gonna make it home tonight.

Pause.

Kelly   Why not?

Craig   I've been trying to get him up for fifteen / minutes –

Kelly   Craig –

Craig   I don't know what else to / do.

Kelly   Wake him up.

Pause.

Call a car, I'll help you get / him –

Craig   – What's the big deal if he just crashes on the couch?

Kelly   *I don't want him here.*

Pause.

Craig   You don't want him / here.

Kelly   I don't want him / here.

Craig   Why don't you / want him –

Kelly   – All right, what's happening?

Pause.

Craig   What?

Kelly   Something is happening –

Craig   So say it then, what?

Kelly   You don't want to be alone with me.

Pause.

Craig   That's not true, Kelly. I'm going to *Iraq*, my brother / is –

Kelly   You're going to *Georgia*.

Craig   – I'm going to Georgia, and then I'm going to Iraq. What, you think I'm being dramatic?

Kelly   Yes, I do.

Craig   – Look, he's not – I don't feel right just throwing him in a car –

Kelly   Why not?

Craig   Because I think – he's scared, and I don't think he should have to wake up alone in the morning / like I –

Kelly   – You keep saying he's scared – we talked about the war half the night, he didn't sound scared at all. He sounded very confident –

Craig   We were talking about politics, not me leaving.

Kelly   – But if he was so scared, I really don't think he would have been able to disagree with you the way he / did.

Craig   That's not even – he was just putting on a show for Tim.

Pause.

Kelly   – What?

Craig   Tim's against the war, so – whatever, the point is, whatever he said / when we were –

Kelly   No, what do you mean, 'putting on a show'?

Craig   Tim's – that's actually not how Peter feels, Peter is not 'against' the war, he was just saying that for Tim's sake.

Kelly   What . . . ?

Craig   He – Peter told me that because *Tim* marches against the war, and because all their *friends* are against it, it's just easier for him to keep quiet about how he really feels.

Kelly   So – everything he was saying – was / just –

Craig   – His feelings are complicated. He's against the administration, but the actual war he thinks is worth fighting. Tim doesn't feel that way, *obviously*, / so –

Kelly   Wait – is *that* what this is about?

Craig   What?

Kelly   Are you acting this way because I agreed with Tim?

Pause.

Craig   Acting what way?

Kelly   Not wanting to be alone with me –

Craig   Kelly, I *do* want to be alone with / you –

Kelly   I could tell you were getting pissed, I just thought it was something to do with Tim. – Is that why you were so pissed off? Because I was / saying that –

Craig   – We *have* never really talked about the war in the terms we did tonight.

Kelly   – Yes we have.

Craig   – *I* recall your saying to me that it would be good for Saddam to be out of power – when the war started. You disagreed with how we got into it, but you felt the Iraqis / would benefit –

Kelly   – What?

Craig   When we watched Tony Blair with Bush, remember? You said how articulate he was –

Kelly   Craig, I said it was a *fake* war that they were *lying* about to get us into –

Craig   You don't remember when we watched Blair?

Kelly   I was – *theoretically*, we were talking about human rights in *general* –

Craig   And I remember you more or less agreeing with me.

Kelly   I was sympathetic – in the *abstract* – to the 'idea' of human rights, I mean, what, did you expect me to argue for Saddam Hussein? Oh, this is ridiculous, you're purposefully / misremembering!

A mobile phone rings once. Both look vaguely to it. Pause.

– Now I'm wondering what *else* I've said to you that you're unclear on.

Craig   What does *that* mean?

Kelly   I'm wondering about our having a *baby* . . .

Pause.

Craig   What about it?

Kelly   I don't know! I thought we were / clear about –

Craig   We just talked about it tonight – when I get back, when I finish / school –

Kelly   In front of *Peter*.

Craig   What . . . ?

Kelly   – *Peter* brought it up, *Peter* asked if we were going to have a baby – were you saying it just to please him?

Craig   Kelly, we've talked about this a hundred times – I want to wait till I'm teaching, I don't want to take any more money from your father.

Kelly   I still don't see what the big deal is –

Craig   The big deal is, he's a *cock*.

Pause.

– Jesus! We talked about starting a family – sitting right on this couch, looking out at the *cloud of death* hanging over / the city –

Kelly   – Please, please don't invoke / that –

Craig   Why not? That day is seared into my – every single thing we said to one / another!

Kelly   – You know what? I'm tired, I want to go to sleep, I'll sleep on the couch – (*Goes to couch.*) Go sleep with your brother.

Craig   Oh, fuck you!

He gets his keys, moves to apartment door.

Kelly   Where are you going?

Craig   For a walk.

Kelly   Craig –

Craig *opens door.*

Kelly   Craig – don't go –

Craig *stops. Pause.*

Kelly   *approaches him. He shuts door. Turns. Pause.* **Kelly** *leans in, kisses* **Craig***. Pause. He kisses back The kiss grows . . .*

Mobile phone bleeps once. **Craig** *looks to it.* **Kelly** *keeps kissing him.* **Craig** *detaches himself and goes to the phone. Picks it up. Pause.*

Kelly   – What?

Craig (*reads*)   'Did Tim leave yet. Horny.'

He looks up at **Kelly**.

Adam.

Pause.

Kelly   – You don't know what it means. It could just be a – like a joke or something.

Craig   A *joke?*

Kelly   Like he teases him by sending him texts like that.

Pause.

What?

Pause.

What?

Craig *looks at the phone again a moment, then puts it down. He gets up, goes to kitchen, opens cabinet, drawer . . .*

Kelly   What are you –

Craig *grabs a pot and a spoon, goes into the bedroom, off.* **Kelly** *stands.*

Offstage sounds of the spoon hitting the pot loudly. After some time **Peter** *comes out of the bedroom. Stumbles. Sees* **Kelly***, smiles.*

Peter   Hey . . . sorry . . .

He grabs jacket, starts to go. **Kelly** *sees phone.*

Kelly   Don't forget your phone.

Peter *(turns)*   Oh – thanks.

He goes to the phone. **Kelly** *moves to bedroom door.* **Peter** *puts phone in pocket, moves to door.* **Kelly** *turns to* **Peter***.*

Kelly   – I think someone might have texted you while you were asleep.

Peter   – Oh.

Pause. **Kelly** *goes into the bedroom, off.* **Peter** *takes phone from pocket, checks it. Then goes out the door, off.*

Pause.

The bedroom door opens. **Craig** *comes out, goes to the couch, curls into it. Grips himself tight.*

Pause. **Kelly** *follows.*

Kelly   Craig.

Pause.

Craig, what's happening?

Moves to **Craig**. *He curls more tightly into himself, burrows deeper into the couch.* **Kelly** *turns and goes back into the bedroom, off.*

Scene Five

Kelly *watches TV.* **Peter** *comes out of the bedroom.*

Peter   Jon Stewart!

Kelly *(turns)*   My other Tivo favorite.

Peter   Yeah, he's funny. But it's weird – I was at a party a couple nights ago? And this guy starts saying Bush is as bad as Hitler. *Then* he starts talking about how hilarious *The Daily Show* is. And I thought – if you were in Germany in the 1930s, would you watch a show where some smartass made fun of Hitler? Little mustache jokes while he's throwing Jews in the ovens? I mean, if you really think George Bush is evil, then how can you laugh at 'George Bush is dumb' jokes?

Kelly   It's the sensibility. The sensibility comes closer to conveying the truth than the real news does, I think that's what people respond to.

Peter   Yeah, but whose truth is being conveyed? Jon Stewart has so much privilege, I think it's a pretty small slice of the 'truth' he's conveying. Like when I watch him make fun of evangelicals – if you really care about the truth, you can't just speak to your own tiny group, you have to figure out how to speak to the community.

Kelly   The community . . . ?

Peter   People who may not be like you but that you still have – something in common with. A basic humanity. Even if they *do* believe in God, or believe in the war in Iraq. Go to

the Indiana State Fair – those are the people we need to
figure out how to talk to. They're not going away, we can't
just make fun of them. Don't you think?

Kelly   But aren't they beyond reach? These people think
the Rapture is coming. They think people like us are going
to burn in Hell – literally.

Peter   But that's the – that was one thing about Craig. He
could talk to those army guys like – it didn't matter,
Harvard, all the books he read – he never forgot where he
came from. He knew that these people, whatever insane
things they believed – he thought you could reach into the
core of them, and find something deeper and truer than all
the surface stuff, God and politics and all that.

Kelly   I don't know – God and politics go pretty deep.

Peter (*mostly conceding*)   Yes and no . . .

Kelly   He thought we could reach the Iraqis too. Do you
think he was right about that?

Pause.

Peter   I hear you. I just don't want to write people off, I
guess. I mean, how do you feel as a therapist? Someone
comes to you with all these problems, doing all these bad
things to themselves, to other people . . . you have to believe
that there's a way to reach them, right? No matter how
awful or crazy they seem . . .

Pause.

Kelly   No, I agree . . . What did your director say? Is
everything okay?

Peter   – I chickened out, I still haven't called him. I was
just leaving messages for my agents, and my manager, and
my lawyer.

Kelly   – Your publicist is out of town?

Peter   I really should have gone to the stage manager.

Kelly   I think you're the last person who needs to be questioning his actions tonight –

Peter   I kind of – I don't know . . . Scott – the director – on opening night – God knows what I was thinking, but . . . Tim had left the party, he doesn't like staying out late – and I was really drunk, and Tim doesn't have much of a sex drive because of the Paxil and – I ended up following Scott into the bathroom – and – honestly – seduced him and – while it was happening, Drew, my understudy, came into the bathroom and saw – Scott blowing me, basically. So . . . I'm sure word got around to the company, I'm sure John heard . . .

Kelly   – Oh.

Pause.

Peter   And – I might as well just put it all out there – I've been sleeping with Adam still. – So, basically, that's my life.

Pause.

You're moving, aren't you?

Pause. **Kelly** *turns off the TV. She looks at* **Peter***, nods.*

Peter   When?

Kelly   Next week.

Peter   Next *week*. Where?

Kelly   I have a good friend from school, in Ann Arbor. She's just been through a divorce. I'm going to go up there for a while.

Peter   What about your practice?

Kelly   I referred everyone.

Pause.

Peter   Why couldn't you . . . did I *do* something that made you not want to talk to me, / or –

Kelly   It's just me. I haven't wanted contact with anybody.

Pause.

I didn't know you were in this much pain, Peter. I'm sorry.

Peter   Oh, it's all – drama. I'm fine, really. I'm so sorry *you've* been – I mean, I figured things were tough, that's why you hadn't . . . I think I had the idea because, just, being in the play made me – I had all these hopes going into it, but it turned out to be like *Long Day's Journey to the Hamptons* – actors constantly checking messages, luxurious spreads of pastries at every rehearsal, Scott taking up all this time telling stories about which Hollywood, actors, have big dicks – I wanted to scream! The play is like being in a *war*, these people are trying to kill each other – literally! My father won't spend money on treatment for my TB, for the sanitarium! And no one was taking it seriously . . . So I sort of – would retreat into my own little world, and read Craig's emails . . . they were so inspiring, I mean, just – this extraordinary thing of him turning against the war, you know? And I kept thinking of the two of you, how much you had wanted a / child –

Kelly   – Turning against the war?

Peter   Yeah – Did you – ? I was wondering if that was something he could even talk about –

Kelly   Not – there were limits to what he could say, he / wasn't –

Peter   So you had no – Oh, Kelly – reading the emails is like – this *awakening*, it's like the birth of this whole other person! I know you said you're not ready – but if you ever do want to read them – just – please – anytime . . .

Kelly   Thank you – I might someday.

Pause. **Peter** *smiles at* **Kelly**. *Looks away.*

Peter   It's late, I should get going. Big day tomorrow, God only / knows –

Kelly   Are you – where are / you –

Peter *goes to his bag.*

Peter   – If you have email in Ann Arbor, I really would like to stay in / touch –

Kelly   – It's late, stay here.

She looks at **Peter**. *Pause.*

Peter   – Okay!

Kelly   – Take the bedroom. In the morning I'll make some pancakes.

Peter   Eeek, pancakes.

Kelly   Oh, right. What can you – I can make them without / sugar –

Peter   Ah, fuck it – pancakes! With *gobs* of maple syrup –

They laugh. Pause.

I'm – glad we could be honest with each other.

Kelly   Me too.

Peter   Yeah. – Just – gonna use the bathroom . . .

He goes into the bathroom, off. **Kelly** *takes the bedsheet off the box and goes to the couch. Sees* **Peter***'s bag. Goes to it, unzips it, looks in. Begins to reach in. Toilet flushes.* **Kelly** *zips up the bag moves away.* **Peter** *comes out of the bathroom, takes his bag.*

Peter   You know – I really don't mind sleeping on the couch.

Kelly   Please – take the bedroom.

Peter   You sure?

Kelly   I'm sure.

Peter   Okay. – G'night.

He moves towards the bedroom.

Kelly   Can I – . . .

Peter *turns.*

Kelly   I think part of my hesitation with – the emails, your asking if you could share them with me before – I think because they were written *to you* I feel – that it's really not / my –

Peter   – Oh, no, I'm *sure* Craig would have wanted me to share them with you.

Pause.

Kelly   Then I think I – I would like to / read them if it's –

Peter   Oh, of course, absolutely. (*Opens bag.*) There's one in particular I've most wanted you to . . . (*Picks one.*) I *think* this is the – they all blur together a little . . .

Sits down, as if to begin reading. **Kelly** *does not move to sit.*

Kelly   – Oh.

Peter   Is it okay if I read it to you?

Kelly   It's not . . . I can read it.

Peter   Oh, you'd rather . . . I just thought it would be – I guess I'm so eager to *share* . . .

Pause.

Kelly   – If you'd – sure.

Peter   Is that okay?

Kelly   Sure.

She sits.

Peter   Okay. If it gets to be too much or anything – just tell me, I'll stop.

Pause. Reads:

'Abu Ghraib is already a punch line; I'll spare you the jokes. For about five minutes we all felt the truth of it but that feeling got swept away in the hot desert wind like every other emotion here.' – A little Faulknerian. 'From what I can tell, it's not a big deal at home either. I think Abu Ghraib would only hurt Bush if it were pictures of Americans jerking off and smeared with shit; as long as it's Iraqis it can only help. There's a real comfort in the images – that we're the powerful ones, in control, alive, clothed. I had a memory the other night of the time Dad put his fist through the car windshield. Do you remember? I can't believe I forgot, and at times I wonder if I made it up somehow. But I recall so vividly Mom telling us when she was taking us to school the next day that it was a Vietnam flashback. We couldn't have been older than six. We were coming back from dinner, Dad was driving, Mom was saying something to him – and suddenly there was a crunch. I looked up and the windshield was like a spiderweb, and there was Dad's bleeding fist, gripping the steering wheel tight . . . I looked over at Mom and I remember thinking that she was going to look a certain way, upset or scared . . . but instead I saw her grinning. A little creeping grin on her face. I looked over at you. You were looking out the window like you hadn't noticed anything, so I punched you in the arm. You said, "Ow," and Dad looked back for a second, then turned back to the road. That's all I remember. I think I've remembered this now, after so many years, because what I learned in that instant – that to be married to a man so powerful he could put his fist through glass was what made our mother smile – is exactly how I feel here: so powerful I can't stop smiling, while suffering a wound I do not feel.'

Pause. He looks up.

Kelly   – Jesus.

Peter   No memory.

Kelly   – You don't remember that at all?

Peter   Vague memory of Craig hitting me and Dad not doing anything. But that happened all the time.

Kelly   – Craig would hit you?

Peter   It was weird. When Dad would hit me, Craig would yell at him to stop. But then Craig would hit me a lot too. When I would go tell Dad, he wouldn't do anything. And when I would go tell Mom she would say, 'Go tell your father.'

Pause.

Kelly   I'm sorry.

Peter   Oh, you know, everyone has a childhood. – Craig told me once – your dad abused you?

Kelly   Emotionally.

Peter   He was never really specific . . .

Kelly   Neither was my father.

Peter   You mean . . .

Kelly   He wasn't around, he was having affairs, he bought me lots of things I didn't want . . . my mother was on too much Valium to care.

Peter   I'm sorry.

Kelly *nods. Pause.*

Peter   Is this okay? Should I / keep –

Kelly   Please.

Peter   It's very eloquent, isn't it?

Kelly   It's beautiful.

Peter   A bit purple here and there . . .

He looks back at the paper, reads:

'The malaise among the men has taken a turn. It's clear to everyone now that we are not equipped to bring this country back to life. The city is dying and we are the ones killing it. Since the mission has no meaning, my men are making meaning for themselves. As you might expect, the meaning they are making is perverse. I can't bear to tell you what I'm seeing. I'm sure you can imagine. All I will add is that it is worse. But I do not blame my men. They were told they would be heroes bringing freedom, and instead have been told to invade people's homes and take their freedom. They are ordered to protect themselves from violence by actively doing violence, which leads to more violence to protect themselves against: no sane person could survive these tasks. I have begun to wonder if I myself will recover from who I have become here, in just a few short months. But then in quieter moments I find myself thrown back into memories of who I was before and am faced with the realization that the horror I feel here is not . . .' Hmm.

Pause.

This sort of goes on for a while, there was a part at the end –

Kelly   No, please, keep reading.

Peter   – Reading out loud, it's longer than I . . . there's a, where is the / part –

Kelly   – Go back, what was he saying about the 'horror' – 'the realization that the horror I feel here'? – I want to hear that.

Pause. **Peter** *looks at the paper.*

Peter   'But then in quieter moments I find myself thrown back into memories of who I was before and am faced with the realization that the horror I feel here is not . . . something I fully understand . . . It is unclear which way the narrative of this war will twist next. Faulkner understood that the psychological legacy of war is that / the individual –'

Kelly   – Are you skipping something?

Peter   No. No.

Kelly   The – read it again?

Pause.

Peter   I think – that part might have been something he meant just for me, actually.

Pause.

Kelly   What are you skipping?

Peter   It's not really –

Kelly *takes the email from* **Peter** *and reads it. She looks up. Pause.*

Peter   I think he – I think he meant just fantasies, or –

Kelly   *Fantasies?*

Peter   He says 'need' – need's not – I mean, Fort Benning was probably anxiety, but –

Kelly (*reads*)   'In quieter moments I find myself thrown back into memories of who I was before and am faced with the realization that the horror I feel here is not just a consequence of the war, but is horror of the core of me, of who I have always been. In fact I have felt more clear-headed here than ever before. I haven't felt the overwhelming need to sexually demean women that has haunted me my entire life, and haven't fucked since leaving Fort Benning.'

Puts down email.

Every night I let him fuck me – every night of my / *life*!

Peter   – I don't – I don't think / he's saying –

Kelly   – Did you know he fucked other women?

Long pause.

Peter   One time –

Kelly   – I knew it –

Peter   – we were – do you want me / to –

Kelly   Yes.

Peter   – we were in a bar, we were drunk, he went to the bathroom – he was gone a while, so when he came back I just said, 'Are you okay?' Like, maybe he was throwing up . . .

Pause.

He said, 'I think the bitch bit me.'

Pause.

Kelly   'I think the bitch bit me.'

Peter   I just thought he / was joking –

Kelly   – I knew when he wouldn't apply for a deferment. I knew –

Peter   – I think it's like, it's the violence just finally got to him, you know? / The –

Kelly   It has nothing to do with – No – he said, it's who he's *always* been –

Peter   No, that's what I mean – like – five years old, Dad took us shooting, there's photo albums of dead animals / all –

Kelly   Don't blame this on your father, it's / not –

Peter   He loved you so much, Kelly –

Kelly   – He was a coward!

Peter   – He fucking shot his head off, right? He obviously felt guilty!

Kelly   Guilt? Over *me*? No, that's not guilt, / no –

Peter   What is it then?

Kelly   – He wanted to get *away* from me!

Peter   – What?

Kelly   He wanted to get away from / me –

Peter   No –

Kelly   – so he went to Iraq and *shot himself – oh!*

She rises.

Leave my house, I need to be alone –

Peter   Kelly –

Kelly *goes into bedroom, off.* **Peter** *stays seated.*

Scene Six

Craig *is on the couch. Near dawn.* **Kelly** *opens the bedroom door, comes out a few steps.*

Craig   Hey.

Kelly   You're talking.

Pause.

Craig   I have to leave / in a –

Kelly   I know what time it is.

Pause. She comes to the couch, sits.

Craig   Get any sleep?

Kelly *shakes her head 'no'.* **Craig** *smiles.*

Craig   Thinking about fucked-her-so-hard-she?

Pause.

Kelly   Why would I be thinking about him?

Craig   You're seeing him.

Pause.

Kelly   No. I am not thinking / about –

Craig   Call the bluff.

Kelly   – What?

Craig   Tell him you know what he's doing. Every time you listen to him go on about one of these women he's getting / off on it –

Kelly   You have never met him. Yes, he is exasperating. But he is a human being, with a history, who is in pain – who is communicating his / pain –

Craig   He's *acting* like he's in pain –

Kelly   – in the only way he knows. He's trying to make me feel small, so I can know how *he* feels: small.

Craig   No, he's just trying to make you feel small. And he'll keep doing it until you crack, and then he'll leave.

Kelly   We have very different views of human nature.

Pause.

Do you love me, Craig?

Pause.

Craig   I don't think we should have a serious discussion right now.

Kelly   Why not?

Craig   I'm not capable of it. I'm stressed –

Kelly   Things have come up tonight. We can't / just –

Craig   I think saying anything is a bad idea.

Kelly   – I think you should be able to answer the question.

Pause.

Do you love me?

Pause.

Did you?

Craig   Did I what?

Kelly   Did you ever love me?

Pause.

Craig   Of course.

Kelly   Of course?

Craig   Of course I loved you.

Kelly   Loved?

Pause.

When did you stop?

Pause.

When did / you – ?

Craig   After we got married. I knew it was a mistake. I knew I didn't love you.

Pause. **Kelly** *cries. She punches* **Craig** *repeatedly. She stops. Pause.*

Craig   I have to get dressed.

Pause. He goes into the bedroom, off. **Kelly** *hyperventilates. Calms some. Picks up her phone, goes to her phone book, dials.*

Kelly   Hi, this is a message for Bradley. It's Kelly Conners calling. I'm sorry to be calling so early and with such short notice. I need to cancel this morning's session. I'm very sorry. I'll see you at our regular time next week. Take care.

Scene Seven

Peter *is on the couch asleep, a script open before him. Bedroom door opens,* **Kelly** *comes out. Pause. She looks at* **Peter**. *Goes into the kitchen and runs water, opens cabinets, makes noise.* **Peter** *wakes up. Sees* **Kelly**. *She sees him.*

Peter   Sorry . . .

Kelly *makes tea.* **Peter** *looks at the box of books.*

Peter   I was looking over one of my speeches – 'It was a great mistake, my being born a man' – I got inspired by all of Craig's books. I must have passed out . . . Melville, Hawthorne, Hemingway, Faulkner . . . I remember in high school Craig was reading *A Farewell to Arms*. He said it was a war novel – I thought it was about a double amputee . . . God, America had so many great writers . . .

Kelly *continues making tea.*

Peter   – Oh, shit, what time is it?

Kelly   Nine.

Peter   Phew – I have a company meeting at ten. Spoke to Scott – told him what happened, he talked to John, John I guess feels terrible . . . Sounds like we'll all kiss and make up.

Pause. He looks at **Kelly**.

Peter   I'm sure this won't make – much of a difference to you, but – I'm really sorry about what happened last night.

Kelly   – Thank you, I accept your apology.

She straightens things up in the kitchen. **Peter** *looks at the couch.*

Peter   I'm gonna miss this couch! I remember, on 9/11 – I had just moved to LA, and I remember calling here, all day, I couldn't get through till late in the night – Craig picked up the phone, and I remember this peace in his voice – telling me about how you two just sat on the couch all day – looking out the window, at the cloud, holding each other . . . When I think of 9/11, that's always the picture I have . . .

Kelly *does not respond.*

Peter   – *That's* what I forgot to ask you! Whatever happened to fucked-her-so-hard-she?

Kelly   – He stopped coming.

Peter   Why?

Kelly   I had to cancel a session, and he never came again.

Peter   Huh. I had this whole fantasy that he was why you changed your numbers, like he was stalking you / or something –

Kelly *stops.*

Kelly   I changed my numbers because of you.

Pause.

Peter   Because of *me?*

Kelly   Peter, you've invaded my home, no warning, you come in here, you / read me –

Peter   I didn't have your numbers –

Kelly   – this email – say what you will, you did it. So please – just say goodbye, and leave.

Pause.

Peter   When did you change them, after getting my letter?

Kelly   I just want to start over.

Peter   I don't understand, what did I do?

Kelly   I just told you: I wanted to start over.

Peter   But – there was no one I could talk to about him, you were / the –

Kelly   There are therapists.

Peter   But – I love you.

Pause.

Kelly   Bye.

Pause.

Peter   *Fine.*

He grabs his bag, starts to go, then stops.

– For you.

He puts the emails down on the couch.

Kelly   How *dare* you – *no*!

Peter *goes, off. Pause.*

Kelly *turns to the window. The sun is shining, sounds of the city coming to life. She looks out of the window.* **Craig** *comes out of the bedroom, in uniform, with luggage.*

Craig   It's time for me to go.

Kelly *turns. Pause.* **Craig** *goes to the couch and sits. He cries.*

Kelly *goes to the couch and sits. After a time:*

Kelly   Listen. I think you were right. I think this stress is – it was a mistake to talk. I don't think this is who we really / are –

Craig   I have to go, I / can't –

Kelly   I know you do. We'll talk when – phone, email, whatever you're most comfortable with, whenever you – we'll find a way to understand what's / happening –

Craig   I don't – I don't think that's a good idea.

Pause.

Kelly   What's not?

Craig   Being in touch.

Kelly   Being in touch . . . at all?

Pause.

Craig   I have to go.

Kelly   Craig –

Craig *rises. He gathers his things and goes to the door.*

Craig   Goodbye.

Pause. He goes, off.

After a time, **Kelly** *gets up and pours herself a cup of tea. She returns to the couch, turns on the TV. Puts on* The Daily Show. *A moment passes. She looks at the emails sitting on the couch. Pause. She picks one up, begins to read.*

She stops, puts it down. Pause.

She goes to the box of books, opens it. Goes to the emails, picks them up. Places them in the box. Sits, begins placing books neatly into the box.

On the television, sounds of Jon Stewart, laughter, applause . . .